A History of Post-War Britain

© PETER LANE 1971

ISBN 356 03252 3

Published by
Macdonald and Co (Publishers) Ltd
49–50 Poland Street
London W.1

Printed by
A. Wheaton & Company
Exeter, Devon

A HISTORY OF POST-WAR BRITAIN

Peter Lane

MACDONALD EDUCATIONAL
49–50 Poland Street, London W.1

Acknowledgements

The photographs and cartoons are reproduced by courtesy of the following:

Camera Press (pages 17, 40, 49, 61, 66, 111, 113, 114, 115, 119, 122, 124, 125, 133, 137, 138, 139, 143, 144, 145, 146, 147, 148, 149); Keystone (pages 9, 10, 11, 16, 19, 27, 30, 41, 42, 45, 50, 51, 55, 58, 63, 74, 85, 89, 96, 97, 125, 129); Paul Popper (pages 11, 44, 48, 50, 65, 67, 77, 79, 93, 94, 121, 123, 127, 134, 140, 141, 143, 149, 150, 151); Radio Times Hulton Picture Library (pages 19, 20, 21, 25, 35, 51, 81); Daily Telegraph (pages 47, 67, 68, 71, 73, 74, 83, 92, 97, 130); Conservative Central Office (page 7); Daily Herald (page 8); Daily Mirror (pages 12, 18, 131); National Coal Board (pages 13, 14, 15); Press Association (page 15); Central Electricity Generating Board (page 17); Labour Party (pages 21, 46, 67); Syndication International (page 22); London Express (pages 23, 43, 69, 91); British Steel (page 26); Ford (page 28); ICI Fibres (page 28); Central Office of Information (pages 37, 38, 52, 100, 102, 136); Imperial War Museum (page 44); Greater London Council (pages 53, 56); Topic (page 54); Marks and Spencer's (pages 59, 127); Glasgow Herald/Evening Times (page 64); The Times (pages 73, 87); Haley's News Photos (page 76); Daily Express (pages 78, 80); W. MacQuitty (page 82); National Association of Schoolmasters (page 91); Mansell Collection (page 98); Inner London Education Authority (pages 99, 101); Henry Grant (pages 99, 101, 103, 152); Hawker Siddeley (page 104); International Business Machines (page 105); British Broadcasting Company (pages 106, 107); British Aircraft Corporation (page 108); British Tourist Authority (page 109); British Overseas Airways Corporation (pages 51, 109); British Railways Board (page 110); Barratt's Photo Press (page 117); Publicity Department, Blackpool Town Hall (page 118); Butlin's (page 119); Swiss Centre (page 120); H. J. Heinz (page 126); Fox Photos (page 128); Council of Industrial Design (page 129); Madame Tussaud's (page 135); Paramount Pictures (page 141); Carshalton Times (page 148); Shelter (page 153)

The maps and graphs on pages 22, 39, 42, 57, 58, 59, 60 and 84 are drawn by Design Practitioners Ltd

Contents

Part 1: the economic and political changes

Chapter 1 Britain in 1945 *page 7*

,, 2 Nationalisation *page 12*

,, 3 The Welfare State – part 1: health and assistance
  page 18

,, 4 The Welfare State – part 2: employment *page 24*

,, 5 The British Empire – part 1: the Middle and Far East
  page 29

,, 6 Rationing and the Festival *page 34*

,, 7 Peace or War? (1945–52) *page 39*

,, 8 Churchill's return 1951–4 *page 44*

,, 9 The new Elizabethans 1953 *page 49*

,, 10 The Welfare State – part 3: housing *page 52*

,, 11 The new society and its new industries *page 57*

,, 12 The classless, affluent society *page 60*

,, 13 The decline and rise of the Labour Party 1951–1970
  page 64

,, 14 The decline of the Conservative Party 1960–66 *page 70*

,, 15 The Common Market *page 75*

Contents

Part 2: some general themes

Chapter 16   The British Empire – part 2: Africa   *page 81*

„   17   The trade unions   *page 87*

„   18   Immigration and emigration   *page 93*

„   19   Education   *page 98*

„   20   Communications   *page 104*

„   21   Entertainment   *page 112*

„   22   Holidaying Britons   *page 118*

„   23   Fashion   *page 121*

„   24   Women and the family   *page 125*

„   25   Crime and punishment   *page 131*

„   26   A youthful society   *page 137*

„   27   Pop music   *page 141*

„   28   The permissive society   *page 146*

„   29   Summing-up   *page 150*

Chapter one
Britain in 1945

Election 1945

In May 1945 the Germans surrendered. The war in Europe was over, and the war in the Far East was drawing to a close. The Prime Minister, Winston Churchill, announced that a General Election would be held on 5 July, to allow the British people a chance to choose a government to lead them through the years of post-War reconstruction.

Most people thought that Churchill, the great Conservative war leader, would win this first post-War election as Lloyd George, Prime Minister from 1916 to 1918, had won the 1918 election. But as Sir William Beveridge, a leading Liberal, pointed out: "At the end of the First War we thought of going back to the good old times. During the Second War we realised that we must go forward and not back, because the times between the Wars were not good." Rightly or wrongly, the people blamed the Conservatives for the troubles of the "times between the Wars" when millions were unemployed [Chapter 4]. They believed that the Labour Party would do better and would be more likely than the Conservatives to put into practice the reforms proposed by Beveridge and others.

On 26 July, after a delay to allow the soldiers' votes from all over the world to be counted, it was announced that Labour had won. Sir William Beveridge called it a "surprising election result. They have acted on the advice which I gave in the first of my campaign speeches in Manchester, that a vote in a General Election was not a vote of thanks to anyone for having led us to victory. They have shown that they wanted Churchill for war, but most emphatically did not want him, or any of his friends, for peace."

Churchill and the Conservatives lost the election in 1945, and again in 1950. However, the great War leader was eventually re-elected Prime Minister in 1951. Here he is seen making an "eve of the poll" speech in Walthamstow East

When the new Prime Minister, Clement Attlee, went to Buckingham Palace, King George VI "could not hide his amazement;" at Claridge's Hotel in Mayfair one lady cried: "It is terrible; they have elected a Labour government. The country will not stand for it."

On the first Wednesday in August 1945 the newly-elected MPs trooped into the House of Lords (their own House had been bombed during the War). The Conservatives cheered Mr. Churchill when he appeared, singing *For he's a jolly good fellow*. The Labour Members sang two verses of *The Red Flag*.

War-damaged Britain

Amid the rejoicing at the arrival of peace, few people noticed what the new Prime Minister, Clement Attlee, said: "We shall have a hard time." Five million homes had been destroyed or badly damaged; factories and ports had been flattened by bombing. Lord Keynes, the leading British economist of the time, reckoned that it would cost about £1,000 million to repair this bomb-damage, and another £1,000 million to replace the machinery, railway stock and other equipment worn out during the War. To repair and replace on this scale meant that Britain would have to import a vast amount of machinery, timber, steel and other materials from abroad.

In the nineteenth century, Britain had been the workshop of the world. When people in foreign countries wanted to build a railway, a harbour, or a textile mill they came to Britain to buy the machinery and materials they required. They also borrowed the money they needed on the London Stock Exchange. By 1939 Britain had lent over £4,000 million to foreign countries. Each year the borrowers had to pay interest on this money, and this interest had paid for about one half of Britain's imports in 1938.

During the Second World War Britain had sold about £1,000 million of her overseas investments, and lost about nineteen million tons of shipping—another source of income. From now on, Britain had to pay for her imports by exporting goods.

The declaration of the Labour victory in 1945. From left to right: Bevin, Attlee and Morrison

Even more serious was the fact that during the War, Britain had borrowed large sums of money from many foreign countries to pay for goods and materials needed to fight the War. The Americans passed the Lease-Lend Act by which they agreed to let the British have what they needed, provided they promised to pay for it after the War. Indian, Egyptian and other governments housed, fed and clothed British troops in their countries, and Britain promised to pay the bills later on. By 1945 Britain owed over £3,500 million to foreign countries.

These debts, and the interest on them, had to be paid by increasing the exports of British manufactured goods—the very opposite of what had happened when Britain had lent money in the nineteenth century. Now Britain had to export goods to pay interest—and not to buy a visible import.

Export drive

Britain had to double her exports in order to import as much as she had done in 1938. But exports could not be increased until factories had changed over from producing war-goods to producing peacetime goods, and until industry was re-equipped and modernised.

American aid

In 1945 Keynes went to Washington, to ask the USA for a huge loan to help Britain to recover from the effects of the War. The Americans lent £1,250 million, most of which was spent in the USA on steel, timber and machinery. By 1947 this money had gone and the country had still not fully recovered. In 1947 the US Secretary of State, George Marshall, proposed that the USA should give even more aid and help the world recover from the War. Two Americans who lived in Britain at that time wrote: "It was Marshall Aid that saved Britain for the Labour Party. This is not to claim that American money was spent on the nationalisation of coal and other things. The money went into food, raw materials and capital equipment. However, it did

London was heavily bombed during the War. This heap of rubble is all that remained of Chelsea Old Church, one of the most famous of London's churches. It has since been re-built

prevent a drastic fall in the British standard of living . . ."

The Board of Trade Journal for 16 October 1948 reported: "Rations of butter, sugar, cheese and bacon would all have had to be cut by over a third and there would have been less meat and eggs. Cotton goods would have disappeared from the home market, supplies of footwear would have been reduced and tobacco consumption would have been cut by three-quarters. It would have meant even less petrol for private motoring and fewer films, newspapers and books. Shortage of timber would have meant a further reduction in house-building, perhaps to 50,000 a year. Most serious of all, our supplies of raw materials for industry would have been affected, and might have brought unemployment figures up to 1,500,000."

The two Americans wrote: "Marshall Aid came in like a lamb on 5 June 1947. Few people—and that went for Secretary of State Marshall himself—grasped the immense possibilities of his statement at Harvard University that Europe "must have substantial additional help." One of the first statesmen to see the vast potentialities of the proposal was Ernest Bevin, who had made an address saying that Britain must "dig for dollars" as she had dug for victory during the War. He knew that the situation was desperate and that the key was the dollar shortage, the imbalance of Britain's trade with the dollar area.

The signing of Marshall Aid on 5 June 1947. From left to right, seated: Cripps, Bevin, Lewis Douglas (US Ambassador) and Douglas Fairbanks. Standing on the extreme left is Harold Wilson

Devaluation

By 1949 British exports were rising—but not quickly enough. The country could still not afford to import as much food or raw material as people wanted [Chapter 6]. In September 1949 the Chancellor of the Exchequer, Sir Stafford Cripps, devalued the pound, in order to help British exports to sell more. The pound had been worth $4.03 and a British car costing £400 sold for $1,612. After September 1949 the pound was worth only $2.80 so that the same car now sold for only $1,120. More British goods would be sold because they were cheaper abroad. As the country earned more foreign currency it could afford to import more, and slowly bring to an end the period of shortages.

Many people thought that devaluation was yet another sign that Britain was no longer a Great Power. In the nineteenth century she had lent money to the world. Now she had to borrow from others. In the nineteenth century the pound was the most sought-after currency in the world; now, although not worthless, it was worth less.

Summary

One American described Britain in 1945 as being "morally great, but economically bankrupt." Britain had led the free world in the war against Hitler; after 1945 she had to pay the price for this leadership. While the Labour government went ahead with its plans for social reform [Chapters 3 and 4], the country's economic position was weak even as late as 1950 [Chapter 6], and even today is weaker than it should be. Because of this weakness Britain was no longer able to rule her Empire [Chapters 5 and 16] or dominate world affairs [Chapters 7, 14 and 15] as she had once done.

Wilson and Cripps in the canteen of the Board of Trade in 1947

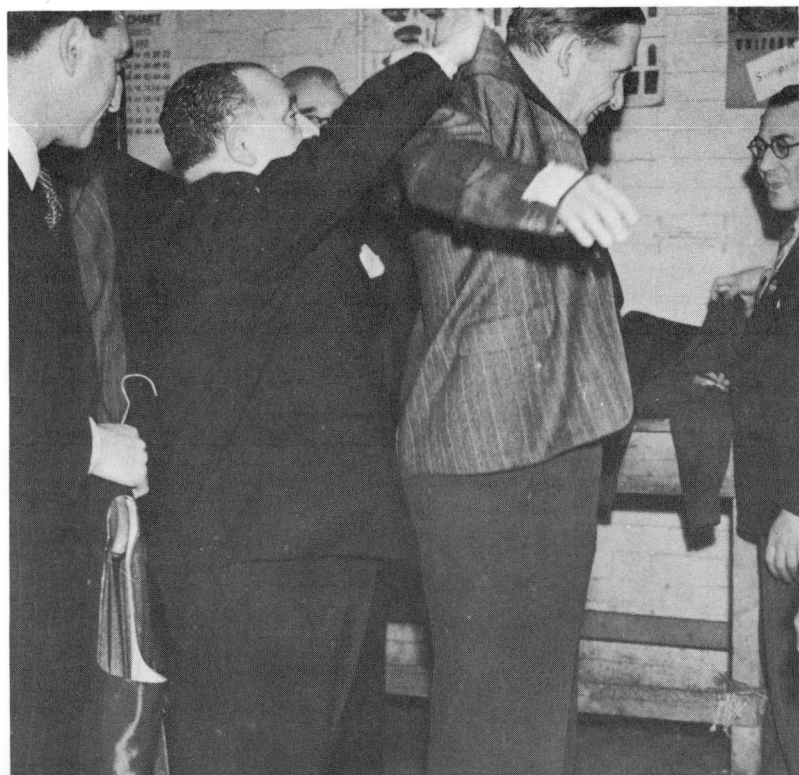

The end of the War: members of the Royal Air Force are fitted out with "demob" – demobilisation – suits. Such clothes were called "civvies" – for civilian wear

Chapter two
Nationalisation

In 1959, Francis Williams interviewed the former Prime Minister, Lord Attlee, for a BBC television programme marking his seventy-sixth birthday. Williams asked: "Had you a complete working pattern of policy already in mind when you became Prime Minister?" Lord Attlee replied: "Certainly. I was determined to go ahead with plans of nationalisation. There were a lot of post-War problems to clear up, but I thought we must push ahead. (It) had to go ahead because it fell in with the planning of the economy. It wasn't nationalisation for nationalisation's sake but the policy in which we believed: that fundamental things must be taken over by the nation as a basis on which the rest of the re-organisation of the country would depend."

The flag of the National Coal Board, which was hoisted at pit-heads throughout the country

Pre-War public ownership

Nationalisation is certainly one of the things for which Attlee's government will be remembered. To nationalise is to take the ownership of an industry out of private hands and give it to the State—as had already been done for the postal services, the BBC (1926), the Central Electricity Generating Board (1926) and BOAC (1939). Even in the nineteenth century many local authorities had taken over the ownership of gas works, water supplies and transport systems. In 1889 a Conservative government decided that private electricity companies would have to hand over their industries to local authorities by 1931.

The Bank of England

The first post-War nationalisation Act (passed October 1945) ended the private ownership of the Bank of England, which then became "the creature of the Treasury" according to Hugh Dalton, Chancellor of the Exchequer. He and many of his colleagues thought that Montagu Norman, Governor of the Bank of England from 1920 until 1944, had been responsible for much of the unemployment of the 1920s and 1930s. Certainly, as Francis Williams wrote: "He was, above all, not moved by science or economics, despising the views of industrialists, trade unionists and economists . . . Throughout those decisive years, British monetary policy was treated as the personal prerogative of a man prepared to sacrifice the economic interests of Britain for those of the City."

On 7 July 1923, the Bank Rate was raised from three per cent to four per cent. This was, said Keynes, "one of the most misguided movements that ever occurred; for prices were falling and unemployment severe and this was bound to worsen the situation . . ."

Keynes was an economist who thought that much of this unemployment could have been avoided—if only the Bank would release the money to be spent on work and provide employment. He wrote: "New capital investment at home would create additional employment. In addition to the men directly employed and to the men occupied in making and transporting the materials required, there will be a further set of men put into work to supply the needs created by the additional purchasing power of the first set of men."

One of the main reasons for nationalising the Bank was to make sure that the money—for investment by government and by private industry—would be available, so that large scale unemployment would be only a memory of the past.

The National Coal Board

The nationalisation of the coal industry received great publicity. The miners had been asking for it for more than fifty years. A Royal Commission had proposed it in 1921. Pre-War governments had gone part way towards it by Coal Acts in 1932,

This headline from the *Daily Mirror* of 1 January 1947 publicises the setting up of the National Coal Board

MORE COAL UP —MINERS DID PULL WEIGHT

BRITAIN'S miners hewed over 500,000 tons more coal during Christmas week than in the corresponding week of 1945, Mr. Arthur Horner, Secretary of the National Union of Mineworkers, revealed yesterday.

"And," he added, "this result was achieved with 4,000 fewer men in the industry.

"These provisional figures justify to the full the claim of the union that the miners would pull their weight. They have done so."

Meanwhile, most of Lancashire's mills are hoping that the workers' New Year holiday today will enable them at least to finish the week without a stoppage due to lack of fuel. Three mills are at present closed.

In Leeds factories the position was easier yesterday. Railway officials said they had had no demands for extra coal trains.

Today the coal mines became the property of the nation.

The hand-over to the National Coal Board will be signalled by the presentation to Mr. Shinwell, Fuel Minister, by Lord Hyndley, Chairman of the Board, of a bound copy of the Nationalisation Act.

Mr. Attlee and other Cabinet Ministers will be present.

Mr. Shinwell, in a pamphlet called "Vesting Day, January 1, 1947," to be presented to all miners, says:

"You are public servants upon whose efforts will depend our future as a powerful industrial country.

"Now We Can Show By Unity"

"Now we can show by comradeship and unity of purpose that this historic event will assist in wiping out the errors and bitterness of the past."

Mr. Will Lawther, president of the National Union of Mineworkers, says:

1936 and 1938. The wartime government had appointed the Reid Committee to examine the coal industry. This Committee recommended the reorganisation of the industry under "an Authority" to be established by Parliament. In the coal industry, as also in the railway industry, too little money had been spent on modernisation and development since before the First World War. Only the government could provide the huge sums required to make these essential industries more efficient.

It was hoped that nationalisation would lead to better working conditions and better industrial relations. Certainly the miners hoped so. From the Rhondda Valley in Wales, a *Daily Herald* reporter wrote: "An hour before dawn today miners' wives took their children, some still asleep, and carried them up the starlit road to the Penallta Colliery to show them something they would remember the rest of their lives. They saw fathers, brothers, cousins, each carrying his lamp, winding out of the colliery yard. A band was playing under the shadow of a pit-shaft. The blue flag of the National Coal Board was hoisted and Bob Silcox, wearing a khaki battledress jacket, shouted into a microphone, "Private enterprise has had it!" The valley rang with cheers."

Coal strike 1947

In May 1947 the National Coal Board introduced a five-day week in the mines, a step towards the "better conditions" for which the miners had hoped. One of the conditions attached to this shorter working week was that coal face stints—the length of coal face that has to be cut on each working shift—should be re-examined. In August two officials of the NCB, accompanied by two representatives of the Mineworkers' Union, visited Melton Colliery, Grimethorpe, Yorkshire and decided that another two feet should be added to the twenty-one feet stints already in existence.

The country needed the extra coal. The miners were now working in nationally owned pits. They had been given their five-day week. But the 104 men at the Melton Colliery refused to work the extra two feet and walked out on strike. 2,500 miners in the Grimethorpe area came out in sympathy with them, and soon 50,000 Yorkshire miners were out on strike, and remained out for five weeks. Thirty-five pits were closed and 600,000 tons of coal were lost.

A miner at work in a wet seam at Canderrig Colliery, an old mine which is now closed

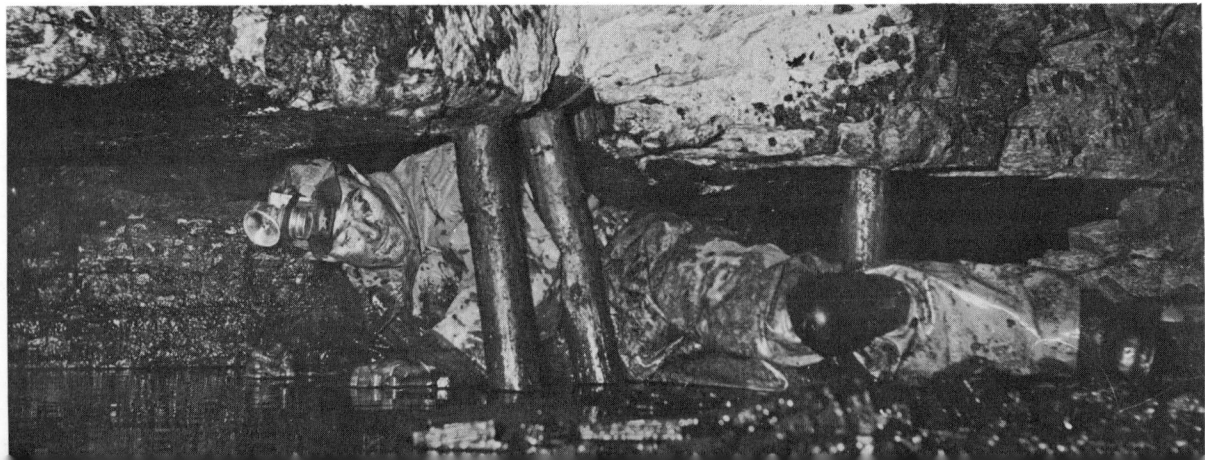

All was not perfect after nationalisation. Here strikers at the nationalised steel works at Port Talbot are seen opposing Vic Feather, the TUC General Secretary, who was recommending a return to work. This was in 1969, nearly twenty years after the nationalisation of the steel industry

The Grimethorpe strike was the first in a long series of strikes in the nationalised industries. The attitudes of the workers and the new managers seemed little different from those of workers and managers in private industry.

Nationalisation—a failure

The workers were disillusioned; so were the customers. Coal was neither plentiful nor cheap after nationalisation. The late arrival of trains became a music-hall joke, although angry passengers arguing with striking drivers failed to see the fun of it.

The taxpayer had been told that the profits from the nationalised industries would be used to pay for such things as social services. This has never happened. The nationalised Boards had to buy out the former owners—the Coal Board paid £164 million to former mine-owners. The Boards have also had to find the money to pay for modernisation schemes and development programmes in the coal, railway, gas and electricity industries. The Boards get their money from the Chancellor of the Exchequer, who collects it from the taxpayer.

So instead of bringing revenue into the Treasury the nationalised industries have cost the taxpayer a great deal of money.

Coal, gas, electricity, civil aviation, transport and the Bank of England were all nationalised in the first two years of the Attlee government. This seems impressive. But the magazine *The*

A miner at work in a colliery equipped with modern machinery. Conditions are far more comfortable and less dangerous than in collieries such as the one opposite

Economist noted: "A Socialist government with a clear majority might well have been expected to go several steps further." One further step which the government decided to take in 1948 was the nationalisation of the steel industry. Morgan Phillips, the secretary of the Labour Party, said: "The battle for steel is the supreme test of political democracy—a test which the whole world will be watching." The steel industry was a manufacturing industry unlike the others that had so far been nationalised. The leaders of the steelworkers' unions, Lincoln Evans and Harry Douglas, were against nationalisation; the Labour government had made no proper plan for nationalisation. When they finally decided to go ahead with the scheme, Attlee asked George Strauss to work out a Bill. It took him a whole year to do so; the Bill was presented to Parliament in October 1948. This meant that the Act was not put into operation until May 1950, when a General Election was almost due.

The left wing of the Labour Party was delighted at the decision to nationalise the steel industry. David Mort, MP for Swansea, said: "We on this side of the House still believe that the earth is the Lord's and the iron ore thereof." But the leaders of the Parties were less sure. Herbert Morrison had said: "Steel nationalisation is not really a Party political matter at all." It became a Party matter in 1948 and 1950 helping the once-jaded and dejected Conservative Party to find a new unity and strength.

It was also the first outward sign that not everyone in the Labour Party still thought of nationalisation as a cure for all economic, social and industrial evils.

The Conservative Party had been only half-hearted in its opposition to other proposals for nationalisation. Indeed, one of their spokesmen, David Eccles, said: "I think today no sensible person would oppose the principle of nationalisation in all its forms." But steel was different—both for the Conservative, and for many Labour Party members, so that *The Economist*

Nationalised British Railways – now British Rail – often suffer from strikes, such as this one, in August 1969. Southern Region train drivers called a lightning strike, which caused chaos in London's rush hour. Here passengers at London Bridge are seen arguing with a crew member of one of the trains

could say in January 1950: "How superficial are the differences between the parties!"

The Labour Party lost the elections of 1951 and 1955, which led some of its members to re-examine the beliefs of the Party. Anthony Crosland, a leading Labour Party authority, argued, in *The Future of Socialism,* that nationalisation had not done what was expected of it, and that private enterprise should be left alone to get on with the job of producing.

The mixed economy

However, the Conservatives, who denationalised the steel industry in 1952, did not try to denationalise the other State-owned industries. On the contrary at times of relatively high unemployment, as in 1958 and 1962, the Conservative governments ordered the nationalised industries to step up their investment programmes, so that employment would be increased. When it was proved that the aircraft building industry was inefficient because there were too many small firms competing with one another, the Minister of Aviation, Duncan Sandys, decided that all the firms would have to merge into two large groups—or face the penalty of not getting government orders. Only one firm refused to obey this order—Handley Page—and this firm was declared bankrupt in August 1969.

It now appears that few, if any, leaders of the Labour Party believe in nationalisation, although the steel industry was re-nationalised in 1969. Equally it appears that few, if any, leaders of the Conservative Party believe in complete freedom for private enterprise. Both Parties have moved much closer together on this, as on so much else. Duncan Sandys organised the merging of companies in the aircraft industry; his successors, in the Labour government, have done the same thing for a number of other industries through the Industrial Reorganisation Commission, which does not nationalise industries, but tries to produce firms which will be large enough to compete with the giant firms of Europe and the USA, and efficient enough to win Britain a place in the economic sun. The Labour Party was once eager to set up Nationalised Boards with Chairmen responsible to Ministers; it now seems eager to encourage the progress of men like Arnold Weinstock who runs the giant GEC-AEI combine.

Arnold Weinstock, a highly successful British businessman, whose huge electrical group merged with Lord Nelson's English Electrical Company in 1968

Ratcliffe power station, near Nottingham, was started in 1963 by the Central Electricity Generating Board, the nationalised body which runs Britain's electricity supplies

Chapter three

The Welfare State—part 1: health & assistance

DO YOU KNOW that all this is part of the Health Service which begins today?
Domestic help where needed on health grounds.
Home nursing for cases needing special care but not suitable for hospital treatment.
Vaccination and immunisation.
Laboratory tests.
Child welfare, health visiting.
Special care after illnesses.
Free use of ambulances.
All kinds of mental treatment.
—AND—

Here are more vital reminders

Mr. Attlee, Prime Minister, last night broadcast these reminders on the new Health Service:

"WHAT we get out of it depends on what we put into our jobs.

"All our social services have to be paid for, in one way or another, from what is produced.

"The general level of production settles our standard of material wellbeing and the real value of money payments into the health scheme.

"There are bound to be some rough edges on such a big scheme to begin with."

It would take time to develop the service, he cautioned. We must start with what we have and work up to a full service when we have got rid of present shortages.

"There'll be Complaints —that's Democracy"

THE Health Minister, Mr. Aneurin Bevan, said at Manchester:

"There will be many complaints about the Health Service during the next few months, because everyone now has the right to voice his complaints about it.

"That is democracy. In the past the distress was there but the complaints were not heard."

Despite our weaknesses as a result of the war, and other difficulties, we now had a moral leadership of the world, he added.

Before many years we would be a modern Mecca to which people would come from all parts of the world to learn how free men, by free institutions, could organise their lives. See "World's Biggest Health Army," on Pages 4 and 5, and "This Day," on Page 2.

This extract about the new National Health Service comes from the Daily Mirror *of 5 July 1948*

On 5 July 1948, the *Daily Mirror* announced: "THE DAY IS HERE! For years the reformers of all parties have tried to safeguard the aged, the poor and the sick. Much has been done. But YOU wanted fuller protection against misfortune. You wanted the State to accept larger responsibility for the individual citizens. YOU WANTED SOCIAL SECURITY. FROM THIS DAY HENCE, YOU HAVE IT." The *Daily Mail* heralded the onset of "A New Britain, a State which takes over its citizens six months before they are born, providing care and free services for their birth, for their early years, their schooling, sickness, workless days, widowhood and retirement. Finally, it helps defray the cost of their departure. All this, with free doctoring, dentistry and medicine, free bathchairs too if needed, for 4s 11d out of your weekly pay packet."

That is how newspapers of different political views welcomed the National Insurance Act, the National Insurance (Industrial Injuries) Act, the National Assistance Act and the National Health Service, all of which came into force on 5 July 1948.

Welfare before 1945

As the *Mirror* pointed out, "much *had* been done." The first Old Age Pension Act was passed in 1908; in 1911 a National Health Insurance Act provided some free medical treatment for manual workers earning less than £160 per year, but not for their families. Everyone else had to pay for medical treatment—for a visit to or by a doctor, for medicine and for treatment in hospital; everyone, including the fourteen million insured workers, had to pay for treatment by a dentist or an optician. Many people were too poor to pay for even essential treatment; in 1939 about six million people wore glasses which they had bought for 6d in the nearest Woolworths.

The War (1939–45) had shown how deficient the social services were. In some places, e.g. London, there were large, well-equipped hospitals; in other places, hospitals had been created out of Victorian workhouses while some places had no hospitals at all. In Kensington, a fashionable and wealthier part of London, there were seven times as many doctors per head of the population as there were in South Shields, in the depressed North-East.

Millions of children were evacuated during the War from city

Lord Beveridge at a discussion of the Beveridge Report at the Central Hall, London, in 1943. On the right is Dr Temple, Archbishop of Canterbury

London mothers with their children about to board the *Evacuation Special* train

slums to middle-class suburban and village homes. Here, for the first time, many middle-class people saw and understood the effects of bad housing and a poor diet. It was this experience that made many millions vote for the Labour Party in 1945 in the hope that a Labour government would change all this.

The wartime government started a National Milk scheme in July 1940 to provide cheap milk for expectant mothers and young children; in 1941 the Ministry of Health provided free cod-liver oil and orange juice at welfare clinics, and in June 1941 Sir (later Lord) William Beveridge was appointed to a Commission to examine the existing social insurance system and to make recommendations for its improvement.

Beveridge Report

Beveridge said: "Now, when war is abolishing landmarks of every kind, is the opportunity of using experience in a clear field. A revolutionary moment in the world's history is a time for revolutions, not for patching." In December 1942 he produced his famous Report which attracted widespread attention. In this he argued that there were five Giant Evils which could affect people's lives: Want (or poverty), Disease, Ignorance, Idleness (from unemployment) and Squalor (from bad housing). He showed how each of these could be overcome by government action. To slay the Giants Want and Disease, he proposed National Insurance and National Health Schemes.

In 1948, both the *Daily Mirror* and the *Daily Mail* welcomed the implementation of parts of the Beveridge Report by the post-War Labour government. James Griffiths, a former Welsh miner, was the Minister of National Insurance who introduced the Industrial Injuries Act—a State insurance scheme to replace the previous unsatisfactory Workmens Compensation Acts. He re-

Outside a pawnshop in 1921. Pawnshops were a common feature of life in the depressed inter-War period. Today, people obtain credit from hire purchase companies

called boyhood memories of buying a 3d raffle ticket to raise money to buy an artificial leg for a miner who had been injured in a mining accident. He also introduced the National Insurance Act. National Insurance was to be compulsory for everyone of working age, except married women. People would pay different contributions, depending upon whether they were employed, self-employed or unemployed. Everyone was to be entitled to insurance benefit if forced to stay away from work by sickness, old age, or unemployment. Everyone was entitled to a retirement pension. There were a large number of other benefits—such as maternity grants, death grants, widows' pensions and guardians' allowances.

Changes since 1948

When the scheme started, employed people paid 4s 11d per week. Increases have been made in subsequent years in the benefits (to cover rises in the cost of living). This has also meant an increase in the weekly payment. In recent years, there has been an important change in the principle of insurance benefit. In April 1961, the Conservative government introduced the Graduated Pensions Scheme, so that retirement pensions would no longer be a uniform, universal benefit but would vary according to a man's income during his working life. At the same time, the weekly payments were changed so that the better-paid worker contributed more than the lower-paid. From October 1966 this "wage-related" system has been applied to sickness, unemployment and other benefits. Thus, a married man with one child, who has been earning £18 per week, now receives £10 12s 6d if unemployed, while a man earning £30 a week receives £14 12s 6d.

National Assistance Board

The Labour government realised that the insurance schemes could not cover everyone. The blind, the deaf or the crippled, deserted or unmarried mothers, and the wives of criminals are not covered by any of the insurance schemes. In 1948, the National Assistance Board was set up to look after such people. The Board provides homes for the homeless and for old people, and can give weekly grants to people with incomes too small to give them a minimum standard of living. Unfortunately, since old age pensions have failed to increase as often or as rapidly as the cost of living, the majority of people applying to the Assistance Board are old age pensioners. In 1966 the Board and the Ministry of Pensions and National Insurance were replaced by the Ministry of Social Security—as Beveridge had originally suggested in his Report.

The National Health Service

The first National Insurance scheme had been introduced by a Welshman, Lloyd George, and improved on by another, James Griffiths. A third Welshman, Aneurin Bevan, was appointed

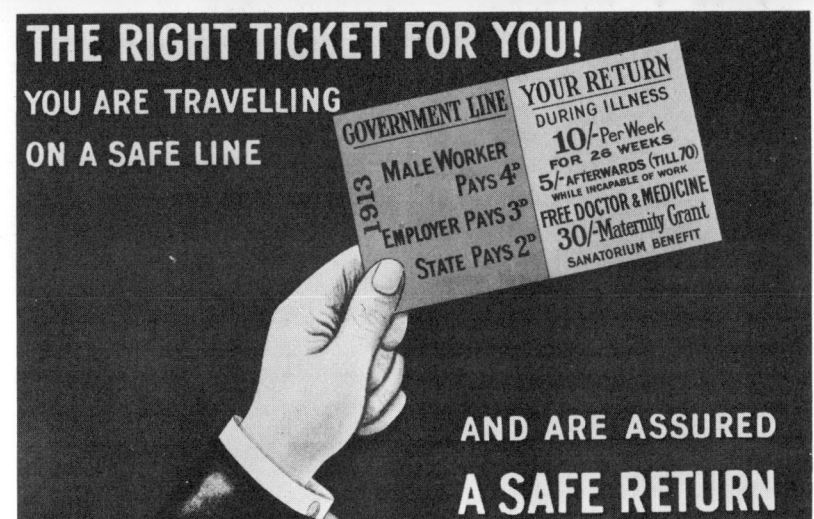

A Liberal Party election poster in 1911, which comments on Lloyd George's introduction of the first National Insurance scheme

Minister of Health in 1945 to introduce the National Health Scheme. Bevan's father had been a founder member of the Tredegar Working Men's Medical Aid Society—an attempt by working men to provide their own health service. Bevan had watched his father die of pneumoconiosis, a disease of the lungs. He was determined to create a Health Service for what he called "my people."

The National Health Service Act nationalised all the hospitals; provided free medical treatment—including the services of dentists and opticians; compelled County and County Borough Councils to provide midwives, home-nurses and health visitors, facilities for vaccination and immunisation, and an ambulance service. Everyone is free to choose a doctor with whom to register so that for the first time there is a "family doctor" for everyone. The doctor is paid an annual fee for every patient on his register—whether he has had to treat them or not.

In 1946 it seemed that the doctors might wreck the scheme. Some of them were frightened that a State Health Service might make them into civil servants, liable to be posted here or there as the Minister decided. Others thought that they might have an

Aneurin Bevan, Minister of Health, after a meeting at the Scarborough Labour Party Conference in 1948

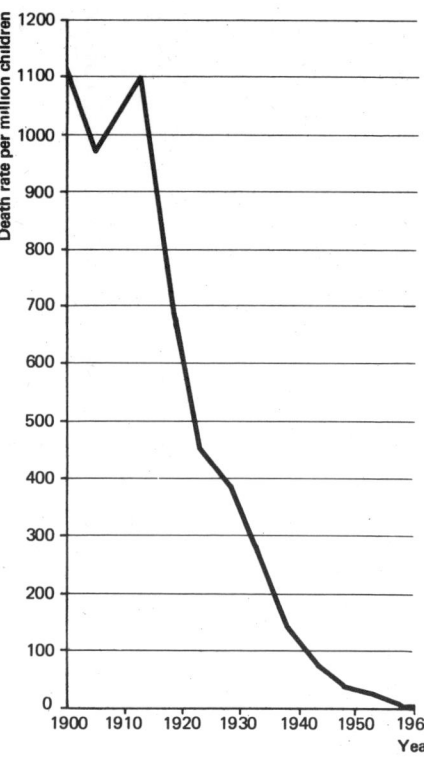

This graph shows the decline of infant mortality in Britain in the twentieth century

official from the Ministry telling them what treatment to give. Very many were afraid that the free system would mean an end to the very well paid private practices that they had enjoyed. Bevan arrived at an agreement with the doctors, who, in the end, refused to follow their leaders' call for a strike.

The cost

The Labour government thought that the Health Service would cost about £140 million a year. However, by 1950, the annual cost was £350 million, and as costs and wages have risen, so the cost of the service has risen each year. In the first two years, (July 1948–July 1950), over 8,500,000 pairs of false teeth were given away, while dentists (paid for each examination, extraction, filling etc.), were earning huge incomes. In Lanarkshire, one dentist earned £25,000 in 1948, and eleven of his colleagues more than £10,000. Seventeen million pairs of glasses were given away in the first two years as people gave up the test-yourself system at Woolworths. Free teeth and free glasses were often accompanied by artificial legs, arms, eyes, surgical boots, invalid chairs and other appliances. The article which fascinated the national Press was the "National Health wig," which could be prescribed for conditions which "would unfit a person for acceptance in normal work or society." One headline ran: "GRANNY, 94, IS GETTING SILVER CURLS FROM BEVAN." "At first I didn't much like the idea," said the old lady, "It seemed like cadging. But so many people seem to be wasting National Health money that it won't do the country much harm if I have my little fling."

A social revolution

Most people agreed with the Conservative, (Lord) R. A. Butler, who said: "I think we should take pride that the British race has been able, shortly after the terrible period (1939–45) through which we have passed together, to show the world that we are able to produce a social insurance scheme of this character."

In this Zec cartoon of 2 May 1946, which appeared in the *Daily Mirror*, Dr Charles Hill, Secretary of the British Medical Association, is portrayed. He had opposed the setting up of the National Health Service. When he called a ballot among the members of the Association, he found that they were overwhelmingly in favour of Bevan's scheme

Cartoonist Low's view of the determination of the British people to create a better future for themselves in the age of Socialism

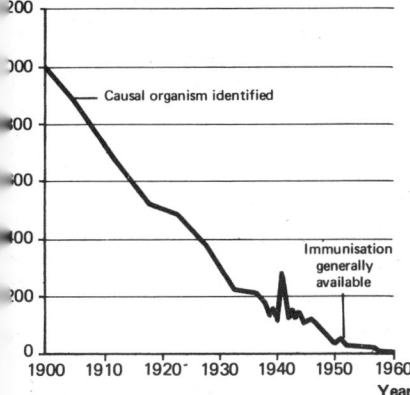

The graph above shows the death rate per million children for whooping cough; the one below for diphtheria

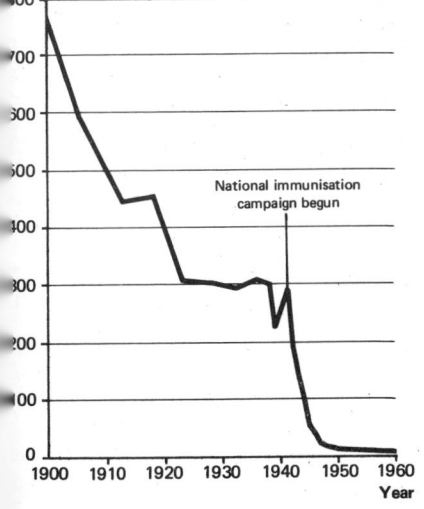

Another Conservative, Robert (later Lord) Boothby, speaking to the Young Conservative Conference in 1949, said that the country had gone through "the greatest social revolution in its history."

Some people had believed the doctors when they claimed that a Health Service just would not work. One man wrote to the papers explaining that up until 1948 he had always paid for medical attention. When he called in a National Health doctor, in August 1948, "I was surprised to find that he behaved just as usual," except, of course, that he didn't have to be paid by the patient.

In 1951, the Labour government was faced with a massive re-armament programme [Chapter 8]. One of the results of this was to force the government to introduce health charges; people had to pay part of the cost of new false teeth and dental treatment. They also had to pay 1s for each prescription they handed in at the chemist's, and a part of the cost of new spectacles. Later governments increased the prescription charges, and although the Labour government removed these in 1964, it was forced by economic circumstances to reimpose them in 1966.

While the *Daily Mail* and the *Daily Mirror* welcomed "The Appointed Day" of 5 July 1948, *The Times* asked: "Can the next generation reap the benefits of a social service State while avoiding the perils of a Santa Claus State?" Many older people think that too much dependence on the State makes the younger generation "soft" and "lazy." An American once told Beveridge that if there had been social security in the days of Elizabeth I there would have been no Raleigh, Drake or Hawkins. Beveridge's reply was: "Adventure came not from the half-starved, but from those who were well-fed enough to feel ambition." Freedom from Want was the privilege of a minority in sixteenth century England; Beveridge wanted this freedom extended to everyone.

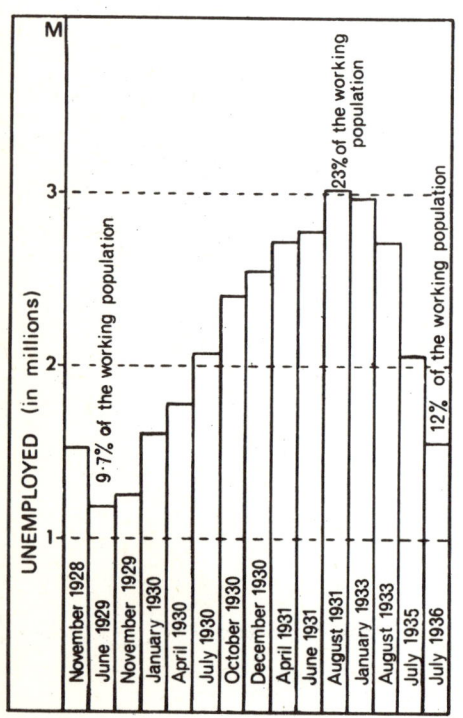

The graph above shows the percentage of workers unemployed in 1934. The graph below shows unemployment figures 1928-36

Chapter four
The Welfare State— part 2: employment

Sir William Beveridge named Idleness as one of the Giant Evils to be overcome in the new society. Indeed he said that Full Employment—the opposite to Idleness—was the basis on which his other recommendations rested. In the affluent society of the 1970s it is, perhaps, difficult to understand this emphasis on Employment and Idleness.

Unemployment in the 1930s

Beveridge and the people who read his Report had no such difficulty. As the graphs show, there were never less than 1½ million unemployed in the 1920s and 1930s, and for nearly three years (1930–33) there were about three million people out of work. The graphs do not show the large number of workers who were employed for only two or three days a week; nor do they take account of the women workers who were not covered by the National Insurance Acts.

Large-scale unemployment covered the country like a grey cloud. But the greyness varied from place to place. The North-East, South Wales and Scotland, where the main sources of employment were the coal, steel and shipbuilding industries, were particularly hit, and suffered more than the Midlands and London, where people were employed in newer and expanding industries, like the car and chemical industries.

Full employment—in wartime

During the War (1939–45) the demand for war goods provided work for millions of people; millions more were conscripted into the Armed Forces. Many women were recruited to work in factories, so that many homes had two or more wage-earners. The War showed that unemployment could be overcome—if the government created work for the people. In a White Paper published in 1944, the wartime government promised to use all its power to see that there was never a return to the large scale unemployment of the 1930s.

Christopher Hollis, a Conservative MP, wrote: "However we may have voted in 1945, none of us looking back can deny that there was at that time a general feeling of disgust in the nation, just or unjust, with the past." One old lady said in 1945: "My son, in the Army, wrote and told me to vote Labour so that he'd have a job after the War."

An out-of-work man on a street corner in Wigan, November 1939. One of the main aims of post-War governments has been to ensure that this does not become a common sight once again

Voting in the shadow of the Pyramids, July 1945. This soldier has cast his vote by post

Full employment—post-War

Since 1945 every government has tried to make sure that the country did not suffer again the horrors of the 1930s. They have tried, firstly, to make sure that there was a high level of employment in the country and, secondly, to move new industries into the depressed areas.

Since 1945, governments have spent millions of pounds on expanding, developing and modernising the coal and railway industries, building new roads, schools, hospitals and houses. Each new investment (or building) means work for a number of people. The government has employed millions of people in the Civil Service, the welfare services and education. It has also encouraged private industry to build new factories and plants which, in turn, have provided work for more millions. Since 1945, the country has had to export more than before the War and this "export drive" has created jobs for many workers.

Full employment—and affluence

Sir William Beveridge had assumed that, even in a good society, there would always be unemployment. He had assumed that at least 8 per cent of the working population (or about two million people) would always be unemployed. Since 1945 the country has rarely had more than 3 per cent of its workpeople unemployed. This very high level of employment has in turn generated a demand for more workers, because the affluent wage-earners have wanted an increasing volume and variety of goods which have had to be produced. John Gunther, an American, visited Britain in the late 1950s. He wrote: "Everybody has money ... Wages have gone up, and never before has the work-

The Abbey Steel Works (Port Talbot) under construction in 1949. This was one of the many post-War developments which provided employment for thousands of workers

ing class had such spending power. When council houses were built, little provision was made for garages. Nobody dreamed that the average working man or labourer would be able to afford a car. So today even the newest housing developments are a tangled mass of parked cars."

People and governments have become accustomed to a level of employment and of affluence never dreamed of in the past. Indeed, the country has suffered from a shortage of workers, in spite of the increasing number of girls and married women who are now at work. In the 1930s there were millions of homes without any wage-earner; today there are millions of homes where there are two, three or more wage-earners.

Inflation

Full employment has brought its own problems of rising wages, rising prices and a deficit on our balance of payment accounts. Some people, such as Professor Paish of the London School of Economics, have suggested that these problems could be overcome if we allowed the level of unemployment to rise, say 3 per cent to 4 per cent. Mr. Macmillan answered such suggestions when he was Prime Minister in 1957, when the affluent society had just begun to appear. He said: "Every Hon. Member knows that for the mass of the people there has never been such a good time or such a high standard of living. I repeat what I said at Bedford, they have 'never had it so good.' I have been grateful to see the change. I believe that all of us in the House, certainly the older Members, feel grateful that there has been this great change. When I am told by some rather academic writer that inflation can be cured only by returning to massive unemployment, I reject that utterly."

Unemployment and Gallup Poll

The winter of 1962–63 was the worst since 1881. The economy had been slack throughout 1962, and the bad weather led to mounting unemployment. The number of unemployed rose to 2.5 per cent of the labour force in December 1962 (compared with 1.7 per cent a year earlier); in February 1963 the total reached 3.9 per cent, the highest figure since the fuel crisis of 1947. The number who feared unemployment was even higher; in December 19 per cent of a Gallup sample believed that they or a member of their family would be affected. The regions farthest from London were particularly hard hit; in February, 7 per cent of the labour force were out of work in the North-East, 6 per cent in Scotland, and 6 per cent in Wales. During the late winter Conservative murmurings against Mr. Macmillan's leadership could be heard.

Redundancy

An industrialised society constantly changes, and inevitably some people will be forced out of work. As the demand for oil or gas increases, so the demand for coal falls and coal miners are unemployed. As more modern machinery is used in steel-making, so steelworkers will be unemployed. Beveridge introduced his scheme of Social Insurance to help the families of men thrown out of work in this way [Chapter 3]. In 1964, the Conservative government introduced a Retraining Act, which set up a number of centres where workers could be retrained. In 1966, the Labour government brought in the Redundancy Payment Act. Previously, when a man was dismissed from his job, the employer did not have to give him any compensation or reward even if he had spent many years with the firm. In future, everyone made redudant (a new word for unemployed), had to receive a lump sum varying with the wage he had been earning and the number of years he had been with the firm. This payment has helped to cushion the blow of unemployment, and helped workers to maintain their living standards while they look for a new job, undergo training, or move to a new area.

Harold Macmillan at the Conservative Party Conference in 1958. He was the Prime Minister most associated with the idea of the affluent society, but he became unpopular in 1962-63 when unemployment rates soared

The new industries moved into the depressed areas. In 1945 the government persuaded ICI to build their first nylon yarn factory (above) at Pontypool, South Wales. This area had once depended on the coal industry; as this declined, so there was increasing unemployment in the 1930s

Depressed areas

It was always hoped that a high level of employment in the country as a whole would make it easier to deal with the much higher levels of unemployment in the depressed areas. If employers found it hard to get workers in the prosperous areas, governments hoped they would be forced to build their new factories in the areas of high unemployment, where there was plenty of labour available. This has in fact happened, although the depressed areas still have higher unemployment levels than the more prosperous parts of the country.

Since the War the government has used its powers to persuade employers to move into the depressed areas. As a result, every firm has to submit plans for expansion to the Ministry of Town and Country Planning, and get a certificate, allowing it to expand, from the Board of Trade. So the government knows of every plan to build or expand. There are various ways in which the government can try to persuade firms to expand in the areas of high unemployment. The government may refuse to issue a certificate allowing the expansion to take place in, say, London. The firm may then be forced to expand elsewhere—or not expand at all. As further persuasion, the government has a wide variety of grants or loans which it can make to industrialists willing to build or expand in an area of high unemployment.

This policy has had a good deal of success: on Tyneside, there are now more people working in new industries than in the older, now declining industries of coal and shipbuilding. Similarly, in South Wales, Hoover and ICI have replaced the Coal Board as a major employer. However, there are still some regions of the country with more industry, more employment and more affluence than others.

Full employment has brought security to millions, and a younger generation with no memories of the 1930s accepts it as natural that there will be work for them to go to. It is also the basis for the affluent society [Chapter 12].

Chapter five

The British Empire—part 1: the Middle & Far East

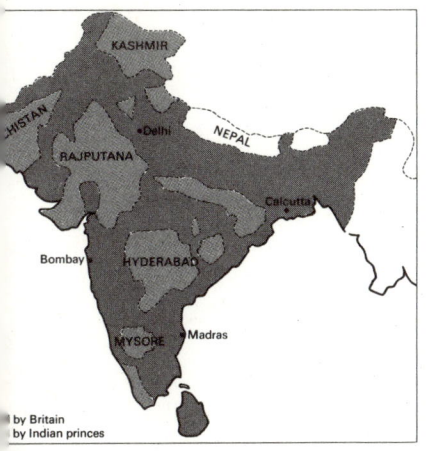

In India before independence (above) and after (below)

Towards the end of the nineteenth century Cecil Rhodes, the founder of Rhodesia [Chapter 16], said: "We are the best race in the world, and the more of the world we inhabit the better." Even as late as 1941 *The Times* wrote: "The moral and material resources of the British Empire are virtually inexhaustible." Since then there has been a great change in Britain's attitude towards, and control over, what was once called the Empire.

The old Dominions

The position of the White Dominions—Australia, New Zealand, Canada and South Africa—had been finally recognised by the passing of the Statute of Westminster in 1931. In 1914 these countries had been independent in internal affairs, but their foreign policies were dictated by the British government. However, the White Dominons demanded independent representation at the Peace Conference in 1918–19, at the end of the First World War, and at the Prime Ministers' Conference (1926), it was agreed that they were in future to be independent in foreign as well as domestic affairs.

India

Disraeli had called India "the brightest jewel in the English crown." By 1914 the British Viceroy ruled over a large part of India with the aid of a Council; the rest of India was governed by independent Princes who were "advised" by a representative of the British government. After 1918 there was an increasingly strong demand for independence for India, but although the British government made some concessions (e.g. giving the vote to most Indians in 1919, as well as establishing a representative system of local government), it was unwilling to give full independence to a country which was torn by religious strife. The Hindu majority dominated the party demanding independence, and although Gandhi, the leader of this movement in the 1930s, promised equality for the Moslems, they and the British were afraid that an independent India might mean ill-treatment of the Moslems. The British government recognised this very real problem, and so did Beatrice Webb who wrote in 1930: "What is as clear as noonday is that though the Indians may not be able to govern themselves they make it wholly impracticable for Great Britain to govern them—if the non-resistance persists and spreads. Neither Great Britain's means, nor her public opinion, would permit any government to reconquer by force of arms. We failed to maintain law and order in Southern Ireland, with three million people, and close at hand; with three hundred million people, far away, the idea is tragically absurd. And we are up against a saint (who) seems potent to destroy the existing order but impotent to create the new."

Lord Mountbatten's mission to India

The Japanese victory over the British in Burma and Malaya increased agitation for Indian independence as well as destroying the idea of British omnipotence. The Labour government which came to power in 1945 had even less ambition and less means than had its predecessors of whom Beatrice Webb wrote. It was faced with too many other difficulties—at home and abroad—to be able to cope with India. Prime Minister Attlee recalls what he did to solve the problem: "Suddenly . . . I thought of Mountbatten. Now, Mountbatten was an extremely lively, exciting personality. He had an extraordinary faculty for getting on with all kinds of people. He was also blessed with a very unusual wife. So I put it to him. He didn't want to drop his naval career. But I talked to him and he very patriotically agreed to take on the job. I saw the King and rather unexpectedly he warmly approved of the idea right away—not everyone would let a member of the Royal Family go and take a risky job, hit or miss, in India as he did . . . He got on the right side of Nehru and he managed to get a joint Government going for the time being with Jinnah (leader of the Moslems) and Nehru and the rest. He got on the right side of Gandhi too, and soon he had all these people talking constantly. And always prominently on his desk to remind them was a card with the date when we would be going (15 August 1947)."

Lord Louis Mountbatten, the new viceroy of India, and his wife, giving a reception for delegates attending the Asian Relations Conference on 2 April 1957. On the right is Pandit Nehru, leader of the Central Government

Riots in India. Part of a mob of two thousand students are shown. They were protesting against the government ban on public gatherings. Police armed with tear gas and staves charged the crowd. Six students were wounded by gun fire, twenty by stave-swinging officers, and three hundred were taken to hospital for anti-gas treatment

Dr Hertz, Chief Rabbi of the United Hebrew Congregations of the British Empire, and founder of Zionism

Indian Independence

In Bombay, Bengal, Bihar and other areas there were violent clashes between Hindus and Moslems, which showed that the separation of the two groups into separate countries was inevitable. The unrest also showed the impracticability of trying to continue the British rule for much longer. At midnight on 14/15 August 1947, the British flag was pulled down in Delhi.

Four and a half million Hindus fled to India; six million Muslims fled to Pakistan. Nearly half a million people were killed or died in the famine which followed. Prime Minister Attlee recalls: "At the end, of course, Winston was strongly opposed ... thought we were being precipitate. The argument always is 'Go slow, and things will get better'." The Dutch and French in Indonesia and Indo-China tried to hold on to their Empires. Bitter and costly wars were required to drive them out. This is what would have happened to the British if they had stayed in India. The Labour government, however, was as willing to accept the change in Asia as it was at home. One result of this has been the goodwill of the Indians towards Britain.

Palestine and the Jewish problem

When the Turkish Empire was split up in 1920, the British government was given control over Palestine. In 1917, the government had promised to set up a National Home for Jews in this area when the First World War ended—it was thought that a few thousand refugees from Russia might make their home in Palestine. At the same time (1915–18), other British officials were trying to persuade Turkey's Arab subjects to rebel against Turkey, in return for which they promised independent Arab kingdoms in Syria and Arabia.

During the 1920s and 1930s, Arab and Jew lived in uneasy peace under British rule in Palestine. Riots were frequent, particularly when the number of Jewish immigrants increased, as a result of Hitler's persecution of the German Jews. Illegal armies and gangs were formed on both sides; both sides fought the British as well as each other. By 1938 the British government was tired of the problem. When the Arabs rejected the idea of a division of the country between the Jews and the Arabs, the government decided that a National Home for the Jews was impossible. Jewish immigration was restricted in spite of the plight of the German Jews.

The Attlee government inherited this along with its other problems in 1945. British was a tired country without the will or the means to maintain peace in Palestine. When President Truman demanded that an extra 100,000 Jews should be admitted into the country immediately, the British government refused, knowing that this would increase Arab bitterness. The Jews entered the country illegally, which involved them in a struggle with both the British and Arab forces. Finally, in May 1948, the government decided that it could no longer cope with the situation and handed it over to the United Nations.

Russian Jews going to Palestine in the 1930s

Persia and oil

In 1951 a new crisis threatened in the Middle East. Britain got most of her oil from Persia, where the Anglo-Iranian Oil Company had been established for many years, but paid only a small portion of its profits to the Persian government. When oil was discovered in Saudi Arabia, the prospecting companies offered the Saudi government 50 per cent of the profits. The Persian government then demanded similar terms as well; in addition, it wanted compensation for all the years during which it had been receiving very little. The Anglo-Iranian Company refused to negotiate on these terms, so in April 1951 the Persian Prime

Dr Mossadeq, Persia's Prime Minister

Minister, Dr Mossadeq, brought in a bill to nationalise the Company's property. In August, the Company evacuated the families of British staff working in Persia, and appealed to the Labour government to stand by the Company. Warships were sent to the Persian Gulf, and for a time it seemed as if Britain might go to war with Persia.

In September 1951 the government decided that the Company's argument was not a sound one, certainly not sound enough to justify going to war with Persia. As Lord Attlee pointed out, such a war would have roused Arab nationalism, antagonised the USA, and would have been no more successful than the Suez War of 1956 [Chapter 16]. So on 3 October 1951, the remaining three hundred and thirty British staff were evacuated on the cruiser *Mauritius*, leaving behind a great refinery and rich oil fields.

The Suez problem

This withdrawal from Persia encouraged King Farouk and his government to oppose the British government. In November 1951, the Egyptians announced their decision to cancel the Treaty which allowed Britain to station troops along the Suez Canal. Once again the newspapers were full of pictures of British women and children being evacuated from a territory which many had always considered part of the British Empire. Again the Fleet was mobilised. Cairo street mobs rioted and attacked British-owned property. Once again the British government was unwilling or unable to do anything about it.

It was little wonder that the *Daily Mail* attacked the Socialist government which had "thrown away India and our greatest instrument in that vast region, the magnificent Indian Army." The *Daily Telegraph* said: "They have surrendered position after position." The magazine *Time and Tide* explained: "When the lion falters the jackals gather," and the *Spectator* said: "An impression prevails in the Middle East that any kind of insolence can be directed against Britain with impunity. This must be stopped without further delay..." But could it be stopped? And if so, how? This was the problem facing the Conservative government which came to power at the end of 1951 [Chapter 8].

King Farouk of Egypt with Mr Bevin, the British Foreign Minister, and the Duke of Edinburgh, in 1950

Chapter six
Rationing and the Festival

Exports and imports

(Lord) Attlee recalled the economic situation which faced Britain when she emerged, morally magnificent but economically bankrupt, from the War (1939–45): "We had to build the export trade, and you can't build an export trade in a vacuum. You've got to have the fuel and the power, transport, finance and all the rest, to do it. And of course because of the export situation, there had to be control of masses of things that were forbidden to our own people at home. Shops would have lovely china— for export only. Very frustrating, but you couldn't avoid it. It was often easier to sell in the home market than the foreign market. To get back into export markets that were essential for our survival, we had to insist that what would sell abroad went abroad."

It was "very frustrating" not to be able to buy things that were being made in factories and and that people could afford now that everyone had a job. Even more frustrating for many millions was the control over house-building. The country needed about three million new houses and yet, Attlee said, "There had to be some control there too. We had to have an allocation of building labour, for example, and materials and so on. The whole thing had to be seen as one. A great deal of industry had been practically destroyed, knocked down; it had to be started again."

It was very difficult for the ordinary person to understand the appeals of Ministers and their learned explanations as to why there was too little of this and none of that. The *Daily Mirror* tried to explain it on January 4 1946, when it said: "The process of turning over from war to peace is proceeding smoothly and quickly. It will mean a certain slackening of 'austerity' at home, but for the present it would be unwise to expect a large flow of goods for individual consumption in this country. The first and essential task which faces the nation is to get on its feet by means of the export trade. To live, to pay our way in the world, we must sell our goods abroad. As industry develops there will be more and more things for the consumer at home."

But the *Mirror* was over-optimistic. A year later, on 23 January 1947, the *Daily Telegraph* headline read:

> "Bread Ration may be cut
> Peers hear Review of 1947 Food Outlook
> Less Bacon and Home Meat
> Beer supplies to be Halved immediately."

Osbert Lancaster's view of some of the problems of post-War Britain. The caption is: "Well, IF Santa Claus had not come out on strike in sympathy with the Euston porters, and IF he isn't subpœnaed to give evidence at the Tribunal, and IF you've been a very good boy, it MIGHT be worthwhile to hang out your stocking as usual." The cartoon appeared on 11 December 1948

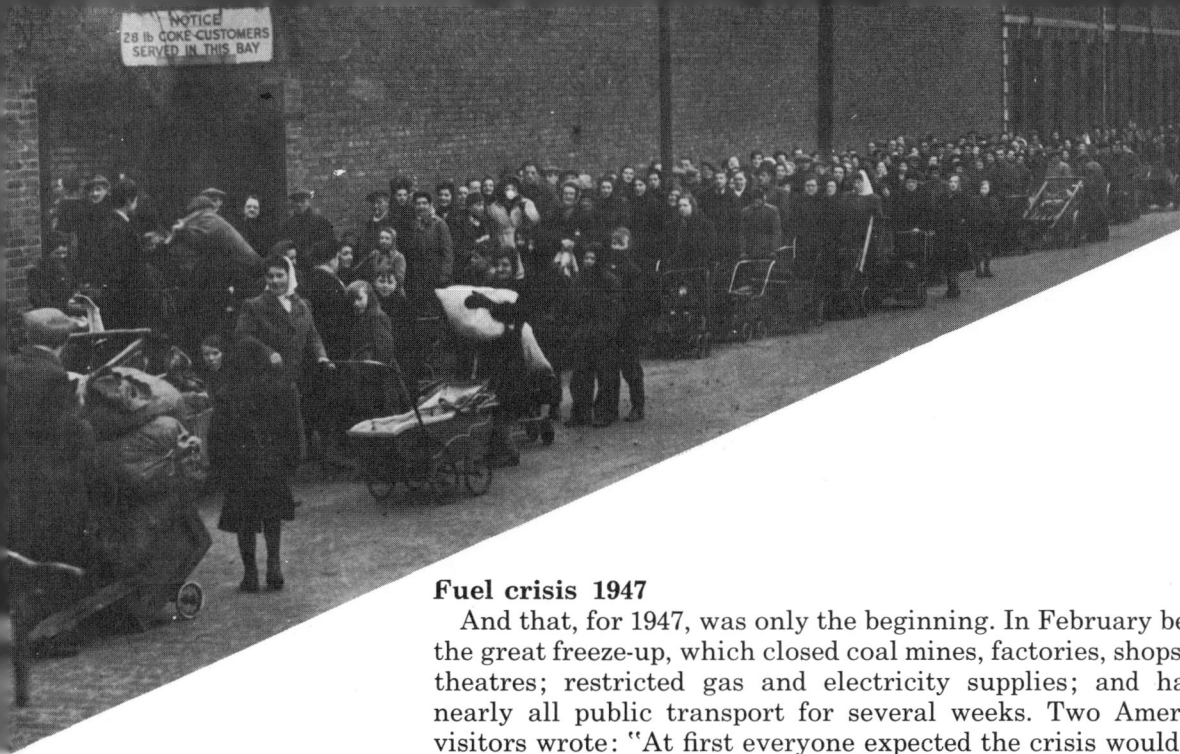

A queue waiting outside Bow Common Lane gasworks, Poplar, waiting to collect coke in February 1947

Fuel crisis 1947

And that, for 1947, was only the beginning. In February began the great freeze-up, which closed coal mines, factories, shops and theatres; restricted gas and electricity supplies; and halted nearly all public transport for several weeks. Two American visitors wrote: "At first everyone expected the crisis would last only a few days but on 8 February there was another heavy snowstorm. By 10 February there were about 2 million men and women thrown out of work. Coal was going only to the larger power-stations, smaller ones closing.

In homes and shops electricity was cut off for five hours daily; the streets of London were almost blacked out. It was depressing to walk along the main thoroughfares of London with their glimmering lights and to see the luxury shops showing their wares by candlelight. The price of candles soared and the shops were denuded of their stocks. That was the period when the city streets were full of gloomy Government posters threatening with want those who would not work.

Greyhound racing, all mid-week horse racing and most matinée performances were banned."

Cartoonist Giles comments on the rationing of bread, which had not been rationed during the War

"Now don't forget—anyone hanging around with a wistful look in their eye—let 'em have it—bing, bang!"

The spiv was a feature of post-War society. This cartoon by Osbert Lancaster, which appeared on 26 June 1947, comments on this type. The caption is: "Don't be so stuffy, Henry! I'm sure that if you asked him nicely the young man would be only too pleased to give you the name of a really GOOD tailor who doesn't worry about coupons!"

Bread rationing

Even during the worst days of the War, bread had never been rationed. But in February 1946 (Lord) Attlee wrote to President Truman of the USA warning him of a world shortage of wheat, and asking the President to do what he could to increase the supply from American farms in order to prevent starvation in many parts of the world. For Britain, he wrote: "We ourselves accept the reduction of nearly a quarter million tons in UK wheat imports for the first half of 1946, although the consequences will be very serious for us. We shall also reduce our fat ration from 8 oz to 7 oz a week which is lower than at any time during the War. This is a consequence of the wheat shortage, since India will have to use for food the ground nuts which she would otherwise have exported to us for fats manufacture. The decision to divert coarse grains from animal to human use will substantially reduce our supplies of meat, bacon and eggs. We have decided to continue our policy of not issuing rice for the civilian population in this country . . ."

Rationing

This is a good example of the attempts by the British government to help the rest of the world, even if this meant sending 400,000 tons of foodstuffs to her former enemies in the British zone of Germany. Prime Minister Attlee thought that the people would understand and be willing to make these sacrifices imposed on them by the need to limit imports. In 1948 a weekly ration list read:

Milk … … …	2 pints
Bread … … …	2 loaves
Meat … … …	1s 6d (although this went down to 8d in 1949)
Cheese … …	$1\frac{1}{2}$ oz
Butter and Margarine	6 oz
Cooking fat … …	1 oz
Sugar … … …	8 oz

Rationing lingered on long after the end of the War. In March 1949 clothes rationing ended—but the meat ration was reduced to 8d worth of meat per person, per week. In May 1950 dried fruit was no longer rationed, but the already scarce cars and TV sets became scarcer as materials were diverted into armaments required for the Korean War. In January 1950 milk rationing ended, but eggs were rationed until August, while meat was rationed until 1954. The whole dreary period of shortages seemed to drag on and on—and not surprisingly the government's popularity fell.

Festival of Britain

The Labour government was trying to be "fair" at home and abroad, and continually urging people to work harder, to pro-

A general view of the Festival of Britain, in 1951

"Contemporary" furniture, displayed in the South Bank Exhibition of the Festival of Britain. Pattern and colour featured, a great change from war-time dullness

duce more, to sacrifice this and that. Many people agreed with Herbert Morrison when he said in 1950 that the people deserved a pat on the back for what they had done, and for what they had suffered in the immediate post-War years. This was his justification for the Festival of Britain. At first this was intended as a commemoration of the Great Exhibition of 1851, but some people saw it as a chance to show the hard-pressed British the new plastics and other materials, the new furniture and colours, the new wall-papers and paints that would soon be available.

After a good deal of discussion, the government and the Festival Committee decided to build a Festival Hall and a display on the South Bank of the Thames, and to open a Pleasure Gardens in Battersea. Not everyone agreed with this decision. Many newspapers asked: "How many houses could have been built with the labour and materials being used here?" The *Daily Express* called it "Morrison's Folly."

On 3 May 1951, the King, speaking from the steps of St Paul's, declared the Festival open—on a grey, drizzling day. However, in the coming months the *Manchester Guardian* wrote: "People making for the South Bank begin to smile as they come close to it . . . on bright sunny days it seems likely that a trip across the Thames will be as invigorating as a trip across the Channel, for in its final form the scene is quite as unfamiliar as any foreign seaside resort." Londoners and millions of visitors from the rest of the country and from abroad poured into the Hall, the Gardens and the Park. When the Festival was ended on 7 October 1951, over eight million people had gone to see this display of Britain's future.

The South Bank was not the only display planned for 1951. There was a Land Travelling Exhibition in the provinces, and another exhibition aboard the aircraft carrier *Campania,* which toured seaside resorts. Towns and cities all over the country held their own festivals. Marghanita Laski, a leading woman author, recalled in 1952: "It *was* nice, wasn't it, last year, Festival Year. It was the nicest thing that happened in England in the whole of my life." Million of others agreed that this escape from austerity and shortage was very enjoyable. It had helped to generate a new interest in design, colour and decoration. A new word appeared in the advertisements—"contemporary"—which was used to describe any and every attempt to get people to abandon old and heavy furniture, and gravy brown and dull green paints.

The end of the Festival in October 1951 coincided with the fall of the once triumphant Labour government, and the return of the Conservative government. David Eccles, the new Minister of Works, was responsible for the demolition of the Festival—all except the Festival Hall.

The Labour Party may have hoped to win popularity with its Festival. But the Festival coincided with great tension from other events, which would have killed any such popularity. Three days before the Festival ended, Persia was finally evacuated [Chapter 5]. As if this was not serious enough, people were beginning to wonder whether the Third World War might not break out at any moment as the Russians fought the USA with her allies in Korea [Chapter 7].

At the end of the Festival of Britain, buildings connected with the Festival were demolished, except for the Festival Hall, which was later enlarged. Here, it is shown in 1967 when two concert halls, the Purcell Room and the Queen Elizabeth Hall, had just been added. They seat 372 and 1,106 people respectively, while the original Royal Festival Hall can take 3,000

Chapter seven
Peace or war? (1945-52)

When the War ended in 1945, everyone looked forward to a period of peace and co-operation between Russia, America and Britain. On his return from the Yalta Conference, Mr Churchill spoke in the House of Commons in February 1945, and said: "The impression I brought back from the Crimea is that Marshal Stalin and the Russian leaders wish to live in honourable friendship with the Western Democracies. I feel also that their word is their bond. I absolutely decline to embark here on a discussion of Russian good faith." Cheers came from all sides of the House of Commons.

Iron Curtain

However, it soon seemed that the friendship between Russia and the Western Democracies had been only a superficial one. As soon as the common enemy, Hitler's Germany, had been

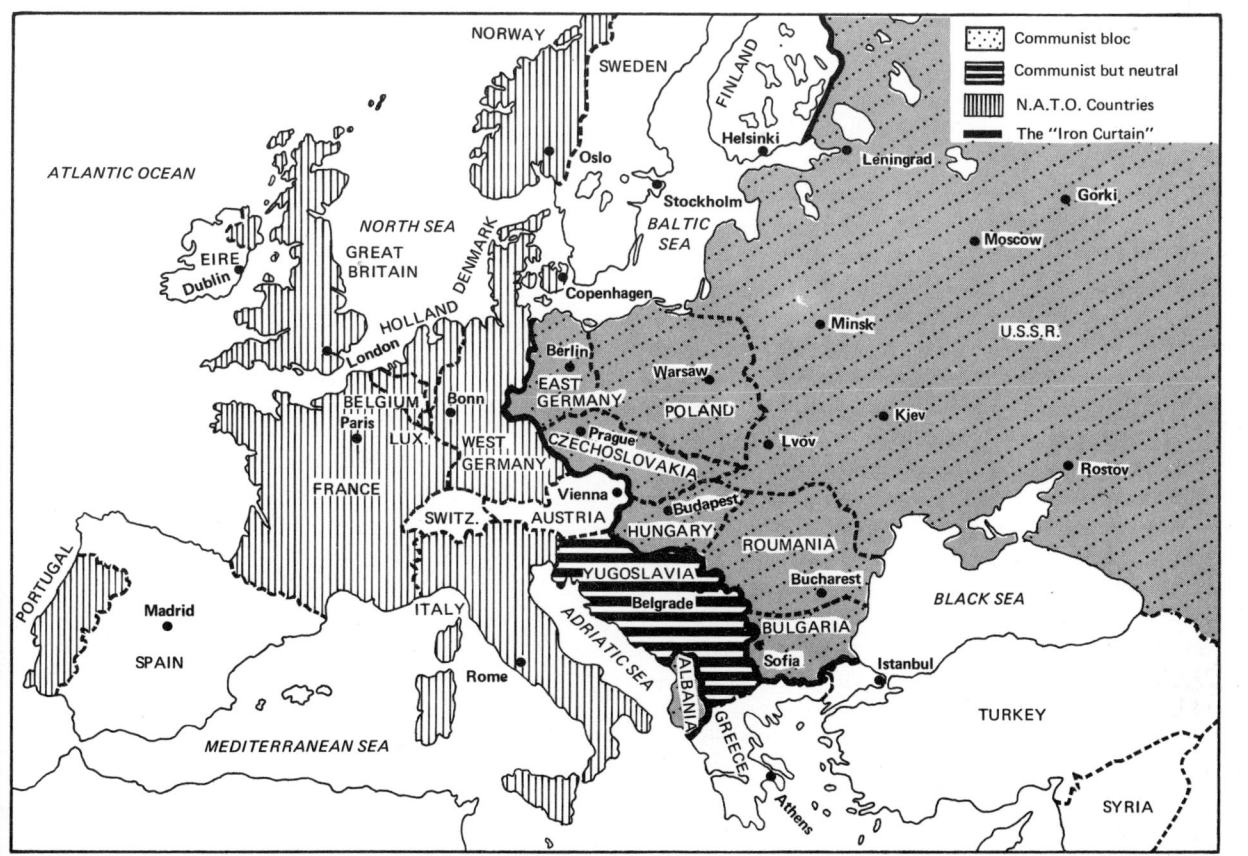

Europe in 1946, showing the Iron Curtain

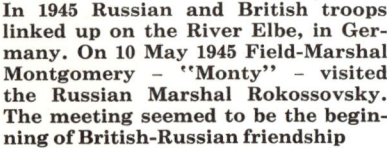

In 1945 Russian and British troops linked up on the River Elbe, in Germany. On 10 May 1945 Field-Marshal Montgomery – "Monty" – visited the Russian Marshal Rokossovsky. The meeting seemed to be the beginning of British-Russian friendship

defeated, old suspicions reappeared. In their drive to conquer Hitler, the Russians had occupied over 200,000 square miles of Eastern Europe, and in the countries they occupied—Poland, Rumania, Hungary, Albania, Bulgaria—they refused to allow free elections to take place, although they had agreed to do so in discussions with the Western Allies. Mr Churchill had had high hopes in early 1945; but speaking at Fulton, Missouri, in the United States, in March 1946, he said: "From Stettin in the Baltic to Trieste in the Adriatic, an iron curtain has descended across the continent."

On the Russian side there was such suspicion and fear of the "capitalist" West that the Russians refused to allow the countries they had occupied to accept American offers of Marshall Aid, even though this would have helped these war-shattered countries to recover, and raise the standard of living of their people. Stalin thought that this Aid was an American attempt to gain influence in Eastern Europe.

This confrontation between Russia and the West was given the name of a "Cold War," to show that while there was great hostility there was, as yet, no *real* war between them. But many people thought, in 1948, that war was very near.

Germany

In 1945 the Allies had divided Germany into four zones, each to be governed by one of the Allies. Germany's old capital, Berlin, was a hundred miles inside the Russian zone, but the Allies agreed it would be a symbol of their unity and of their victory if this city, too, were divided between them. The Russians allowed the Americans, British and French to use certain roads, canals and railways across the hundred miles of their zone to reach their respective zones of Berlin—with soldiers, supplies etc.

In 1948 the three Western Allies decided that the time had come to help the Germans rebuild their country. They allowed free elections in their zones, and as part of a programme of economic reform, introduced a new monetary system. Stalin saw

Occupied Germany and Austria: Berlin and Vienna were under four-power control, Bremen was in the US zone. Each zone rapidly became governed according to the wishes of the occupying power. In the case of East Germany, this became permanent

German recovery as a threat to Russia. He thought the Allies were rebuilding Germany in order to use her power against Russia in a future war. When the Western Powers issued the new currency in their zones of Berlin, the Russian retaliated by cutting Berlin off from the West. All road, rail and canal links were closed; Berlin was to be isolated from the West; the Allied Powers were to be shown that they could not stay in the city.

Berlin Airlift

General Lucius Clay, then in charge of the American zone of West Germany, said: "When Berlin falls, West Germany will be next." So it seemed to many people. So began the Berlin Airlift.

Day by day the job of supplying two million Berliners with coal, food and other necessities went on. At first there were only a hundred transport planes available, but soon the operation had built up until it seemed like an aerial invasion with aircraft landing at the rate of one every five minutes.

The Truman Doctrine

The Airlift ended in September 1949 and marked a major turning point in the policy of the US government, which had already begun to play a large part in European affairs. The Marshall Plan was one proof of this. Another was the Truman Doctrine, by which the American government agreed to supply Greece and Turkey with materials and money to help them resist the threat of Russian agression and Communist guerila force. But the American people were suspicious of all this. Some thought that Truman was being misled by the British. Prime Minister Attlee was asked: "What would you put as the turning point as far as American policy was concerned?" "The Berlin Airlift. I think that was the decisive thing. Of course they'd begun to realise earlier that they couldn't just stand out . . . we (had) made the Americans face up to the facts in the Eastern Mediterranean. As a result we got the Truman Doctrine, a big step. (But) it wasn't, I think, until the Berlin Airlift that American public opinion really wakened up to the facts of life. Their own troops were involved in that, you see. Before that there'd been a lot of wishful thinking. In spite of everything I don't think they really appreciated Communist tactics until Berlin."

Loading planes to take part in the Berlin Airlift

A United Nations Police Force in action for the first time. These Danish soldiers wear a blue UN armlet and blue UN steel helmets. They are about to board Swiss aeroplanes to go to Egypt

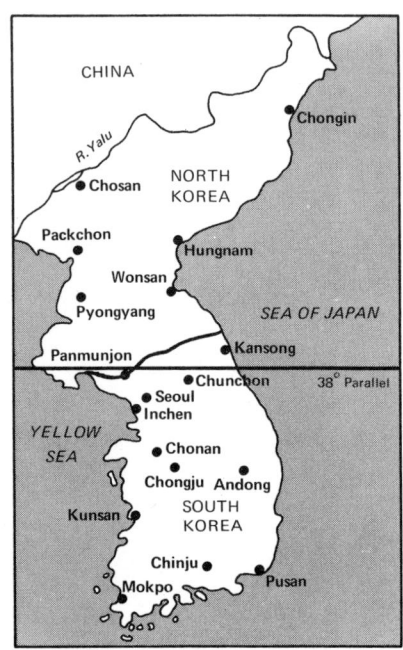

NATO

In April 1949 the North Atlantic Treaty Organisation was established. This consisted of the USA, Britain, France, Belgium, Luxembourg, Canada, Denmark, Iceland, Norway, Italy and Portugal, and aimed at containing Russia within the boundaries of 1948.

Soon after this, in September 1949, it was announced that: "His Majesty's government has evidence that within recent weeks an atomic explosion has occurred in the USSR."

Until then only the USA and Britain had known how to make the atomic bomb. Now that the Russians had it, many feared (with Professor Einstein) that "General annihilation beckons." Added to the threat of Soviet tanks and divisions, there was now the atomic bomb.

Korea

Soon after this announcement, on 1 October 1949, Mao Tse Tung became the Chairman of the People's Republic of China as Chiang Kai Shek's army was finally driven off the Chinese mainland. Communism had made yet another major gain. Many people in the West feared that Russia and China would together conquer the world. This fear was deepened by events in Korea.

Korea had been part of the Japanese Empire. In 1945 the Russians and Americans had divided it between themselves, taking the 38th parallel as the boundary. The Americans wanted free elections and the formation of a government for the whole country. The Russians refused, and in 1950 there were separate governments in North and South Korea.

On 25 June 1950 the North Korean Army invaded the South. To many this seemed like Russia's answer to the American policy of containment in Europe; if Russia were to be held back in one place, then she would strike in another. The Americans took the issue to the United Nations Security Council from which, for some months, the Russians had been absent, as a protest against the American refusal to accept Communist China as a member of UNO. This absence was fortunate, as it allowed the Americans to push through their proposal that a United Nations army should be sent to help the South Koreans. The bulk of the army was supplied by the United States, although small contingents of troops from Britain, Turkey and other UN countries, and some ships of the Royal Navy, were sent out.

At first the invaders from the North swept all before them, and the UN forces were pinned in a narrow coastal area around Pusan. However, on 15 September 1950, the UN Commander—General MacArthur—organised a successful seaborne attack on Inchon, which was quickly captured. Within days the better-armed Americans had recaptured Seoul, the capital of South Korea, and had cut the invaders off from their supplies in North Korea. When the Americans had reached the 38th parallel, MacArthur announced plans to occupy North Korea, uniting

Mao Tse Tung, now famous for the *Thoughts of Chairman Mao*, in 1943

the country under an American-supported government.

The Indian government warned the Americans that an attack on North Korea would make the Chinese even more hostile to America. It was the American fleet which prevented the capture of Formosa, where Chiang Kai Shek ruled; it was the American veto which prevented Mao's government taking the Chinese seat in the UNO. The invasion of North Korea would be seen as the build-up to an attack on Red China itself.

However, on 24 November 1950, General MacArthur announced an "end-the-war" push to the Chinese frontier. He promised that the troops would be "home by Christmas." Four days later, 300,000 Chinese soldiers crossed the frontier into Korea, and the Korean War was no longer a police action against North Korea but was a major war against China. The Chinese drove the UN armies back beyond the 38th parallel, and it seemed as if they might throw them back into the sea.

General MacArthur wanted to bomb the railway lines and assembly yards inside China; he even talked about using the atomic bomb. President Truman agreed at a Press Conference that "the use of the atomic bomb was under active consideration." Members of the House of Commons were staggered at this report and were delighted when Mr Attlee announced that he was going to fly to Washington to persuade President Truman not to use "the bomb." The newspapers were equally delighted. "ATTLEE WILL FLY SUNDAY" said the Saturday's evening papers; "TRUMAN WILL BE AT AIRPORT" said Monday's *Daily Express;* "ATTLEE ON LAST LAP" said the early editions of Monday's evening papers. "TRUMAN GREETS ATTLEE" said the late night final papers.

The meeting was successful. General MacArthur was sacked by President Truman. An armistice was signed with the Chinese in June 1951, although a peace treaty was not signed until 1953. For the time being, at least, the danger of the Third World War was over.

This cartoon by Low shows Mr Attlee meeting Mr Truman

Chapter eight
Churchill's return 1951–54

A wartime ration book

Clothes rationing ended in March 1949. This photograph shows Harold Wilson, then President of the Board of Trade, symbolically tearing up a book of clothing coupons

Rearmament

The Korean War had a profound effect on life in Britain. The Labour government announced that every young man would have to do two years' National Service in one or other of the Armed Forces. This was part of a massive re-armament programme whereby Britain was to spend £4,700 million over three years to try once again to become a first-class military power, able to face the Russians and the Chinese. This programme meant that men and materials had to be diverted from producing consumer goods (such as cars and TV sets) to producing weapons. This cut in the British standard of living was not unnaturally resented by many people, so soon after the end of the War.

Britain has to import most of the raw materials she requires to manufacture goods for consumption at home and for export abroad. When the Korean War started, the USA was afraid that this might be the start of a long war with Russia and perhaps China. To make sure that they would have enough raw materials (copper, zinc, tin, lead, wool) for such a struggle, the US authorities tried to buy up as much of the world's supply of these essential raw materials as possible. This American stockpiling drove up prices, and British importers had to pay more for the raw materials they wanted.

Rising prices

This increase in import prices led to an immediate increase in the cost of living in Britain. Everything that was imported—timber, wool, oil, rubber, even food—became dearer; and manufacturers passed on the increases to the consumer. The trade unions had agreed, in 1948, to help the country's economic recovery by not asking for wage increases as long as prices were held steady. By the middle of 1950 prices were rising so rapidly that the combination of stable wages and rising prices led to a fall in the standard of living of wage-earners. In 1950 the unions told Sir Stafford Cripps, the Chancellor of the Exchequer, that the wage freeze would have to end, and unions would have to be free to get higher wages. Britain was faced with a new problem—rising prices (inflation).

Rearmament—the bill

The government had to find the money to pay for the rearmament programme. Part of the money was found by increased taxation—income tax, petrol and purchase tax. But part of the money was found by using existing taxes to pay for rearmament. The government had to cut down on some of the things it had set out to do (e.g. no new hospitals were built), and people had to pay for things which they would otherwise have got for nothing. From 1951 on people had to pay part of the cost of dental treatment and for spectacles; and there was a charge of 1s for each prescription handed in at a chemist's.

Labour Ministers' ill-health

The Labour government that faced the crisis brought on by the Korean War had lost the confidence it had shown in 1945. Ernest Bevin had been taken seriously ill in April 1950. Attlee was reluctant to take Bevin from the Foreign Office, but early in March 1951 "he was suffering intensely. It was heartbreaking having to tell Ernie he must move out but there really wasn't any choice." On 14 April 1951 this giant of the Labour movement died.

Harold Wilson leaving Number 10 Downing Street with Sir Stafford Cripps, Chancellor of the Exchequer, in 1950. Later that year Cripps resigned from the government for health reasons

This was not the first nor the only loss. Sir Stafford Cripps resigned after writing a letter to Attlee in October 1950: "My doctors here have now completed their examination . . . unless I go off for a prolonged rest I shall probably do irreparable harm to my health. Under these circumstances I see no alternative but to hand in my resignation." Six years of government had taken their toll on the Prime Minister himself who was in hospital when he received Aneurin Bevan's resignation.

The Labour government splits

The debate on the 1951 Labour Budget, while Attlee was still in hospital, was described in the *Manchester Guardian* as a "picture of a government suffering severe internal bleeding and likely to bleed to death at any moment. For the greater part of three hours, Labour members got up one after another to attack each other. The Tory Opposition might not have been part of the House of Commons."

The budget was introduced by Cripps's successor, Hugh Gaitskell. One of those who resented his promotion was Aneurin Bevan, who described him as a "dessicated calculating machine." During the budget debate Bevan wrote to Attlee: "The Budget is wrong because it is based upon a scale of military expenditure which is physically unattainable. It is wrong because it foresees rising prices as a means of reducing consumption. It is wrong because it is the beginning of the destruction of those social services in which Labour has taken a special pride. I am sorry that I feel it necessary to take this step . . ."

Hugh Gaitskell took over from Cripps as Chancellor of the Exchequer. He put forward his first budget proposals on Budget Day, 10 April 1951. Here he is seen with the Budget Box

The Daily Telegraph

GENERAL ELECTION SUPPLEMENT

SATURDAY, FEBRUARY 25, 1950

RESULTS AT A GLANCE

the Government	Old House	New House	Against the Government	Old House	New House
OUR	367	296	CONSERVATIVES	203	268
OUR-CO-OPERATIVES	23	18	NATIONAL LIBERALS AND ASSOCIATED GROUPS	16	16
			ULSTER UNIONISTS	10	10
	390	314		229	294

Independent Non-Government Parties

RALS (previously 10) 8   COMMUNISTS (2) ... 0   LABOUR INDEPENDENTS (6) ... 0
IRISH NATIONALISTS (2) 2   INDEPENDENTS (9) ... 0

LABOUR MAJORITY OVER CONSERVATIVES 19

LABOUR MAJORITY OVER ALL PARTIES 10

[The Speaker, who is non-party, is not included in these figures.]

TOTAL			
CTORATE	33,579,253	FOR THE GOVERNMENT	13,178,787
ES CAST (Not yet complete)	28,196,314	CONSERVATIVES	11,236,413

Results Outstanding 6
Including One Deferred Poll, in Manchester.

The figures at the top of the page relating to the Old House of 640 members are inclusive of seven Labour seats vacant at the Dissolution.

An extract from the *Daily Telegraph's* General Election Supplement of 25 February 1950

Bevan's resignation was followed by that of the youngest member of the Cabinet, Harold Wilson. Attlee said: 'I was surprised when Harold Wilson took Bevan's line. He ought to have had more understanding of the economic position."

In February 1951 an American admiral was appointed to be supreme Commander of the North Atlantic Treaty Organisation Fleet—which included the British Home Fleet. "I do not think that our country ought to have fallen so low," said Mr Churchill in the House of Commons.

The Empire given away, the £ devalued, the Navy controlled by Americans, continued rationing and restriction—it was not surprising that in February 1950, at the General Election, the Labour government's majority was reduced to only five. The *Daily Mail* said: "WELL, THEY'RE IN, BUT FOR HOW LONG?"

The reorganised Conservatives

In 1945 Hartley Shawcross had claimed: "We are the masters ... for a very long time to come." The Conservative Party, under Winston Churchill, had been shattered at the election. But within six years it was back in power again. The Labour Party's defeat in 1951 was partly the result of the Korean War, of the quarrelling within the Labour Party itself, and of a general

Mr Churchill won the Woodford (Essex) constituency for the Conservatives in the 1950 election. Here he is congratulated on his victory by Lord Woolton, wartime Food Minister

feeling of disatisfaction with the continued shortages. But it was also due to the Conservative Party's success in re-organising itself. Lord Woolton became chairman of the Party Organisation in July 1946. He raised £1 million, appointed a large number of Party Agents in important constituencies, and founded the Young Conservatives. Within three years the Party, which had seemed shattered in 1945, was alive again. Under the leadership of R. A. Butler, the Conservative Party Research Department was strengthened. Young men such as Enoch Powell, Iain Macleod and Reginald Maudling hammered out new policies for the future. With Quintin Hogg and Peter Thorneycroft, they produced a series of documents explaining how the Conservative Party would improve life in Britain when it returned to office.

The main difference between the Parties was that the Labour Party talked of controls and planning, while the Conservatives stressed the abolition of controls and "Setting the People Free." As they pointed out, there were few controls in the USA, where private enterprise was producing a high standard of living and enough surplus wealth for the USA to support Marshall Aid and the Truman Doctrine. It was argued that private enterprise would have the same effect in Britain, and people wanted a change after so much austerity.

Conservative government

In October 1951 Attlee called another election; he felt that he could not carry on with a majority of five. The result was a victory for the Conservatives. The headlines read: "WINNIE IS BACK. THE LION LIFTS HIS HEAD." But for the moment life in Britain went on much the same. In mid-November the Conservative Chancellor, R. A. Butler, announced that Britain was in danger of being bankrupt, idle and hungry, so that further import cuts, reductions in rations and tax increases were unfortunately necessary. On one of the most popular radio programmes, *Take it from Here,* the comment was: "Have you seen Jimmy's new suit? It's a conservative cut." "What's a conservative cut?" "It's the same as a socialist cut, only they're more polite about it."

Chapter nine
The New Elizabethans 1953

The Festival of Britain came to an end in October 1951 as the Conservative government took over from a tired and badly split Labour Party. But in the post-Festival year, it did not seem that a change of government meant any real change in the facts of economic life. The country was still on the verge of bankruptcy.

King George VI

In September 1951 King George VI had a lung operation. There was some anxiety about his condition, but as the winter wore on he had recovered sufficiently to take a holiday at Sandringham. His daughter, Princess Elizabeth, set out on a five month long tour of the Commonwealth. But on Wednesday 6 February 1952, at 11.15 a.m., a special edition of the London papers appeared on the streets. They were black-bordered and read simply: "It was announced from Sandringham at 10.45 a.m. today that the King, who retired to rest last night in his usual health, passed peacefully away in his sleep early this morning." The news came as a shock to Britain and the world. In the republic of India, which no longer owed any allegiance to the Crown, newspapers appeared the next day with black borders around their edges. In South Africa people knelt and prayed in crowded shops. In the USA the anti-British *Chicago Herald Tribune* carried a simple but sufficient headline: "THE KING IS DEAD."

This historic photograph shows, from the left: King George V and Queen Mary (seated); the Duke of York (who succeeded his brother Edward VIII as King George VI in 1937); the Duchess of York (later Queen Elizabeth) with the fourteen-month-old Princess Elizabeth on her knee; the 14th Earl of Strathmore, and the Countess of Strathmore, parents of the Duchess of York. The photograph was taken on 27 July 1927.

Queen Elizabeth II arriving in England after breaking short her tour of the Commonwealth. Churchill and Attlee came to meet her

Edmund Hillary, conqueror of Everest

Queen Elizabeth II

The young Queen came home from Kenya to take up her new position, and was met by Mr Churchill and Mr Attlee both of whom had served her father. Coronation Day was fixed for 2 June 1953. Five weeks before that date Queen Mary, the new Queen's grandmother, died. She had been crowned in 1910, when Britain was truly great. Two World Wars and forty-three years later, her granddaughter was to be crowned Queen of a poorer Britain and of a smaller Commonwealth.

The Coronation made a considerable impact outside Britain. Christian Dior, the French fashion designer, said: "The Coronation of the young Elizabeth II has filled not only the British, but, rather strangely, the French too and much of Europe with renewed optimism and faith in the future."

Only a handful of people were in Westminster Abbey to see the young Queen crowned, but over twenty million people watched the ceremony on BBC television. This was indeed the first monarch ever crowned—as the prayer-book demands—"in the sight of all the people."

The conquest of Everest

On Coronation morning the newspapers carried the story of another drama—the conquest of Everest. Several earlier expeditions had tried to climb Everest, but none had succeeded until on 1 June 1953 (Coronation Eve) a British team under the leadership of Sir John Hunt reached the previously inaccessible peak.

Falling prices

Sir Gordon Richards rode the Queen's horse to victory in the Derby following the Coronation, in front of the Queen and a million racegoers. The Korean War came to an end and there was a rapid fall in the price of raw materials as the Americans stopped stock-piling. This fall in import prices was one of the main reasons for the improvement in British living standards in the 1950s. In a BBC discussion with (Lord) Attlee, Francis Williams said: "I have heard it argued that if the 1950 election had been delayed and our general economic position had been given opportunity to develop, you might have got a sufficient working majority in 1950 to make the 1951 election unnecessary. In that case Labour would still have been in office when the terms of international trade turned in our favour after the Korean War ended and it became possible to take controls off and ease things all round—which might have altered the course of politics considerably—indeed there might still be a Labour government (in 1959)." Francis Williams realised that there was a close connection between falling import prices, growing British affluence, and the popularity of the government which happened to be in power when this change took place. Attlee's reply was brief: "That's all very conjectural."

In newspaper articles and radio programmes the young Queen Elizabeth II was compared with the young Queen Victoria.

Queen Elizabeth II leaving Westminster Abbey after her Coronation

The *Comet*, BOAC's new plane. Its first scheduled flight, on 2 May 1953, was a sign of the new Elizabethan age

Prosperity 1955. Television sets, refrigerators, washing machines, holidays abroad and other hints of the affluent society to come were in the reach of many workers in Britain's booming industries. This photograph shows customers in the Household Department of Selfridges

People wondered whether this might be the start of another period of greatness for Britain. Historians wrote learned articles on the theme. "The signs are bright for a great revival." The staff artist of the *Daily Express* "as a stimulant to your understanding of history" recreated a large tableau of New Elizabethans including ballerina Margot Fonteyn in a farthingale, inventor Frank Whittle in doublet and hose, and poet T. S. Eliot wearing a ruff.

Falling taxes

In keeping with the theme of "newness," R. A. Butler, the Chancellor, introduced a "New Look" budget for 1953. He took 6d off income tax and 25 per cent off purchase tax to show that the days of austerity were over. The new economic age had begun. For fourteen years there had been full employment, and most people had money to spend—but little to spend it on. For seven years, since the War, British industry had been working at an unprecedented rate, but most of its production had been needed to rebuild a war-devastated country or for export. But in 1953, as the prices of imports fell (and exporting became a little less vital) some of the super-charged capacity of British industry could be released to produce goods for sale at home. The affluent society was just around the corner.

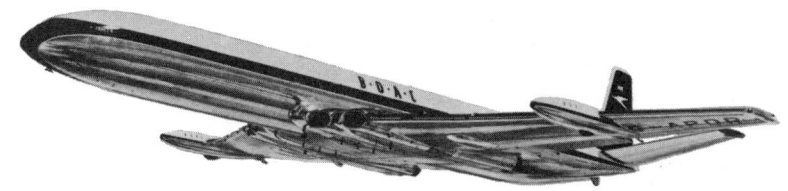

Chapter ten

The Welfare State— part 3: housing

In his Report (Lord) Beveridge named Squalor as one of the Giant Evils to be overcome by government action. He wrote about the cramped and squalid conditions in which millions of people lived in Britain's old towns and cities. He pointed out that the schemes for a better Health Service (and healthier people) and for a better education system could not work unless there was also a State-aided scheme for better housing.

New Towns

In 1944 the government proposed that fourteen New Towns should be built around London. These would not be large housing estates like those on the outskirts of towns in the '30s, but completely New Towns where people would both live and work.

In 1946 the Labour government passed the New Towns Act which set up ten Development Corporations, each of which was to establish a New Town. The Development Corporation, with government money, bought the land required for a town of 50 or 100,000 people. Architects were appointed to plan and build the New Towns, with shops, cinemas, halls, factories, offices and houses for families of different sizes. In improving old towns the architects and planners have to take into account the cost of land, and compensation for the owners of shops and houses that will have to come down if the planner's dream is to

The town centre at Harlow, one of the fourteen New Towns proposed by the Government in 1944. This photograph was taken in 1968

come true. In the New Towns there were no such problems; the architects were completely free.

In 1952 the Conservative government passed a Town Development Act, which gave government money to small towns which agreed to absorb "overspill" populations from large cities. Worsley, in Lancashire, was already taking in overspill population from Salford. Wolverhampton Council had already made arrangements for Walsall to take some of its growing population. After the passing of the 1952 Act, Bletchely, Aylesbury, Swindon and Basingstoke became overspill towns for London; and a number of other expansions were planned.

New life

For people leaving a pit-valley in South Wales to live in Cwmbran, or for Londoners leaving a Stepney slum to live in Harlow, the change was like emigrating to a new country. Encouraged by their new surroundings and by full employment, people bought new furniture, equipped their kitchens with refrigerators and washing machines, and in general agreed with Harold Macmillan's verdict "They have never had it so good."

Britain's older industrial towns had grown in such a way that poor people tended to live in one part of the town, the better-off in another. Each group or social class had its own churches, schools, societies, and often its own shopping centres and parks. In the New Towns there was a greater mixing of classes in churches, schools, societies and clubs, and in the New Towns we can see the first signs of that "endless middle-class" society which David Butler discovered when making a survey before the 1959 General Election: "A New Town resident could even tell an interviewer: 'There aren't any poor now . . . Just a few . . . in London'."

This is the society where everyone thinks they belong to the middle class. It is a society which owes more to Simon Marks (of Marks and Spencer's) than to Karl Marx.

Squalid conditions in an old house in Paddington, London

A family re-housed in a modern flat

Squatters leaving a block of luxury flats in Kensington, London, 20 September 1946

Cartoonist Low's idea of the immediate future facing post-War Britain. With so much to be done to the wrecked world, it is not surprising that, for a time, there were shortages and difficulties

The homeless

But for many millions of people the 1946 New Towns Act meant nothing. Many thousands had been made homeless by bombing, and millions were living in the three million houses which were already over a hundred years old in 1945. Many had no bathrooms, no toilets and too little space.

Aneurin Bevan, Minister of Health and Housing in the Labour government, understood the connection between good health and good housing, and was anxious to rehouse as many people as possible. However, Britain's economic position in 1945 meant that only a limited amount of timber could be imported. Some of this was needed for new factories and schools, so that only 200,000 houses a year were built between 1945 and 1950. Even so, the total of a million new houses was more than any other European country built in the same period.

Council housing

Nearly all these houses were built by councils and were for rent to people who could not afford to buy their own houses. Each council opened a Housing Department, and people who wanted a council house put their names on a waiting list. In an attempt to be fair, a system of housing points was invented: people on the waiting list were given so many points for the number of years they had been on the list; so many for the number of people in the family. This meant that young, newly-married people went to the bottom of the list; it also meant that people who were high up on a list or who had just got a new house were unwilling to move—even if unemployed—to an area where they might have got a job, because they knew they would have great difficulty in finding a house.

The Squatters—1946

In the summer of 1946 thousands of people all over the country, tired of waiting for a house, took the Law into their own hands. They put their belongings in prams or in handcarts, left the one

AND NOW TO WORK

Even in the 1970s there are families living in run-down houses such as these

or two rooms in which they had been living and set up home in Nissen huts on old Army camps. By early September 1946 Squatters had become part of national life. On Sunday, September 8, London saw the Great Sunday Squat. From Stepney, Hammersmith, Westminster, Wembley, Hendon, Wandsworth, Croydon, came hundreds of homeless people to occupy luxury flats in Kensington and Marylebone—which had been occupied by the Services but which were waiting for redecoration before they were handed back to their former owners.

Electricity, gas and water supplies were cut off, and at night candles and oil lamps shone from the high windows. The Communist leaders of the London Squat were arrested, and eviction orders were issued by the Courts against the Squatters. Within ten days they had packed their pots, pans and children into their prams and had gone. But they had shown how desperate was the need for housing. The government set about rehabilitating old Service camps and soon there were 563 makeshift villages, housing over 6,000 families.

Housing boom

The fall in the price of raw materials after 1953, and the improved economic situation, meant that more men and materials could be used for housing. The Tory government announced that it would build 300,000 houses a year, but that unlike the Labour government, it would allow the building of houses for sale. By 1958 over 10 million people were living in houses built after 1945. For very many people a new house, like the New Town, was the beginning of a new life.

The improvement of housing conditions in the last decade is one of the most potent factors in the transformation of the working man's way of life. A shop-steward, who had been living for two years in his own modern house, observed: "In the previous house the front door was never meant to be used; we had a settee across it. Everyone, including the postman, called at the back door. Now it is different. We've moved to the front." That "moving to the front" has a deeper meaning. It stands for the shedding of the old-fashioned workmen's sense of inferiority. A man's wife on a new estate told an interviewer how the old kitchen was gradually losing its appeal as the centre of the family: "In the other house the front room was never used except for Christmas. If I lit a fire in the front room we always seemed to get back into the kitchen. I suppose we were used to it. Now it's different." TV has also contributed to this change in which one can say that the kitchen mentality is gradually being replaced by the livingroom mentality.

In 1956 the government announced the end of the "subsidy" system; previously, the government had given councils a grant for each house that was built for rent. This had meant that the council had to pay less than the real cost of the house out of its own funds. It also meant that the rent that the council charged was less than had it would have been without this subsidy. Since 1956 government grants have been given to councils only for houses built as part of slum clearance schemes.

Private housing

Many councils now decided to build fewer houses, because they did not want to find the extra money out of the rates. But houses were still built at a rate of about 300,000 a year. Now, however, more and more of them were built for sale, and, in the increasingly affluent society, more and more were bought by working class people. A survey in 1960 showed that over a third of new houses, and over half of old houses sold that year, were bought by wage-earners. Surveys taken at large factories at Birmingham, Workington and Luton showed that between a third and a half of the workers owned their own houses.

Many others lived in houses which they rented from private landlords. Since 1917 various Rent Control Acts had stopped private landlords increasing their rents, so that many houses fell into bad repair because their owners could not afford to pay for improvements. It also meant that tenants had become used to paying low rents which took a decreasing proportion of their increasing weekly wages.

In 1957 the Conservative government passed the Rent Act which freed from rent control any houses paying more than £40 a year in rates. It also laid down that new tenants moving into a house after the Act was passed could be charged any rent by the landlord, which led to the development of Rachmanism. Rachman was a London landlord who owned big, old houses which he let out in separate rooms to many tenants. His tenants were often poor, but their rents were controlled. Rachman, and many other landlords, like him, had no power to evict them, but got rid of many by threats. When he had driven them out he could legally put new tenants in at uncontrolled rents.

One of the first Acts passed by the new Labour government in 1965 was a Rent Act which restored most of the controls that had been abolished by the 1957 Act, provided security of tenure so that tenants could no longer be evicted by their landlords, and set up Rent Tribunals to which tenants could appeal if they thought their rents were too high.

By 1965 over five million new houses had been built in Britain since 1945, but every year more old houses were falling into disrepair, houses were being knocked down to make room for road-widening schemes or other developments. Every year the demand for houses grows as more people get married at an earlier age than in the past. The New Towns have been built, but the old industrial towns of the North, Scotland and South Wales have not disappeared. In 1966 it was reported that three million people were still living in slum houses. For these, the affluent society has little meaning. It is something that they read about, but do not share in.

New council flats at Roehampton, London

Figures for crude steel production

Chapter eleven
The new society and its new industries

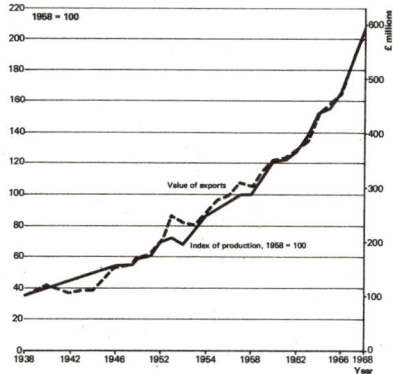

Figures for the production and export of chemicals

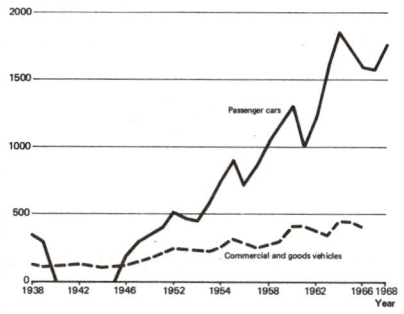

Figures for the production of motor vehicles

New industries

In the nineteenth century the cotton and coal industries were the foundations on which Britain's economic strength had been built. Since 1945, these old industries have been in decline; fewer people now work in them and they contribute a smaller share to the country's income than they did in the past. But newer and larger industries, such as the chemical industry (dominated by Imperial Chemical Industries), the motor-car industry (with large firms such as Ford and British Leyland), the aircraft, engineering, oil-refining, synthetic fibres, pharmaceuticals, plastics and electronics industries, have all grown very rapidly in post-War Britain.

These industries produce things as different as Rolls-Royce aircraft engines and hair oil, but they have many things in common. Most of the firms in these industries are very large, employing many thousands of people—unlike the small, family firms which started off the Industrial Revolution in the nineteenth century. Often, one or more of the large firms tries to become even larger by buying other firms in the same industry. William Morris started to build motor-cars before 1914, and founded Morris Motors which became one of the largest British car-producing firms. In 1962 his firm joined with Herbert Austin's firm to become the British Motor Corporation, and in the late 1960s BMC joined with Leyland to form British Leyland. The same sort of development has taken place in most of the other new, growing industries.

These large firms are owned by shareholders who have little, if any, control over them. The important decisions are made by chairmen or managing directors most of whom are themselves only employees of the firm which they control. Many of the largest firms in Britain are partly or wholly owned by even bigger American firms, e.g. Ford, Hoover, Vauxhall, Esso.

All the large firms have very large administrative staffs at a head office. In the 1930s William Morris was quoted as saying: "All the organisation is in there"—tapping his head. Today, British Leyland has to employ thousands of designers, research workers, clerks and salespeople. So do all the other large firms, which explains the building of so many large office blocks.

The use of an increasing amount of machinery has taken a good deal of the dirt and sweat out of work. On the building site the hoist has replaced the hod carrier; on the railway the driver

A self-service launderette, an example of one of the new service industries, which made life easier for many women

This graph shows the number of employees in selected industries in Great Britain

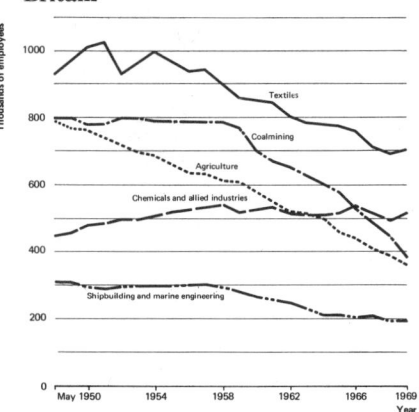

and his companion no longer shovel coal; in the docks the fork lift truck has made the life of the dockworker much easier. In the newer industries this is even more true; in the machine shops the skilled and semi-skilled workers have replaced unskilled "labourers."

Industries and education

The growth of these new industries has been a major reason for the increasing demand for better education. Five per cent of ICI's work force have university degrees, and an even higher proportion have some paper qualification. The same is true in most scientific-technological industries. The increasing demand for educated workers had meant increasing opportunities for young people to climb the promotion ladders, so earning more money and becoming socially mobile. John Gunther once noted: "It would be a gross exaggeration to say that class distinctions in England no longer exist—but it is nowhere nearly so important as it was. Before the War if a boy's father was a coal miner the chances were that the youngster would follow him; only exceptionally gifted, aggressive or lucky people emerged from their environment. But today young men and women climb out of their backgrounds with comparative ease."

New shops

The increasing output of these new industries has to be sold, or they will grind to a halt. Side by side with the new industrial revolution there has been a retailing revolution. In the 1930s the great departmental stores (e.g. Harrods, Selfridge's and others in London, Lewis's in Manchester), had been a symbol of national prosperity. In the 1950s and 1960s the symbol of an even greater prosperity was the growth of the chain stores, which were opened not only in the big cities but in the High Streets of every large town.

The outstanding examples of the new chain store is Marks and Spencer's—founded in 1884 as a "Penny Bazaar"—an apt reflection of the spending power of the mass of the population in 1884. Even in the 1930s Marks and Spencer's was "respectable" but "lower class." In the 1950s and 1960s it was transformed, under the direction of Simon (Lord) Marks and Israel (Lord) Sieff, into the model for every other chain store in Britain. In Marks and Spencer's the docker's wife and the doctor's wife buy from the growing range of good quality, mass-produced goods. There are few families in affluent Britain which do not wear some of the products sold in Marks and Spencer's. Beveridge and Attlee had asked for "Fair shares for All"; Marks and Spencer's provided the clothes for the "All".

More goods and more money

"Half our trouble in England," said Ernest Bevin, "is that we suffer from a poverty of desire." In the 1950s and 1960s this

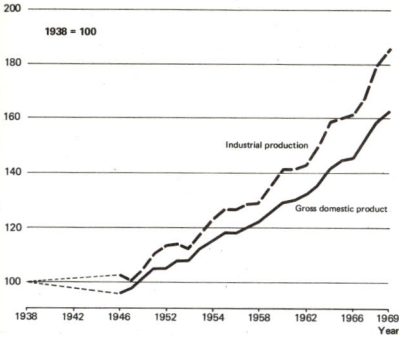

The graph above shows productivity: output per man in Great Britain. The one below shows output per man-hour in selected countries for manufacturing industries only

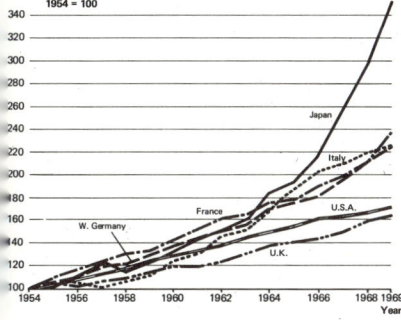

Busy shoppers in a branch of Marks and Spencer's

"poverty" came under attack from the increasing output of the consumer goods industries, from advertising on TV and in the Press, and from the re-designed shops of every High Street. In the five years up to 1960 there were more changes in the shopping scene than in the previous fifty. Shoe shops became glittering places; the windows of the radio and electrical shops were filled with the symbols of the new society—washing machines, refrigerators, cookers and TV sets.

During the 1950s the Conservative government dismantled the Socialist system of controls. Rationing ended in 1954, subsidies on food and house-building were ended by 1956. The Rent Act freed housing from government control. In 1951 the Tory election cry had been "Set the People Free." They had done so, and in 1957 Mr Macmillan, the Prime Minister, could rightly say in the House of Commons: "I repeat what I said at Bedford: 'They have never had it so good'." In 1959 the Tory election manifesto was: "Conservative Freedom Works."

Chapter twelve
The classless, affluent society

In 1931 Professor R. H. Tawney, a famous historian, wrote: "The Classless Society is one in which while occupations and incomes varied, people would nevertheless live in much the same environment, would enjoy similar standards of health and education, would find different positions equally accessible to all of them, would be equally immune from the more degrading forms of poverty." In the 1930s the Marxists claimed that Russia was just such a society. Britain certainly was not, as John Gunther recalled [Chapter 11].

However, in 1952 Professor Tawney wrote: "England, a pioneer of religious and political equality, has known little of economic and social (equality). Her history (has) supplied no experience by which to judge the effects of her recent, unspectacular turn towards (economic and social) equality." Even as early as 1952 he could see that Britain had taken "a recent and unspectacular turn" on the road towards equality and the classless society. Since 1952 the British have taken longer strides along that same road.

Higher incomes

One of the main reasons for this change between 1931 and 1952 (and since), has been the high level of employment. Beveridge thought that at least 8 per cent of the labour force would be unemployed, even in his "New Society." In fact there has never been more than 3 per cent unemployment in post-War Britain—except during crises such as the fuel shortage of 1947 and the hard winter of 1962. An increasing number of well-paid jobs have been provided by employers willing and able to pay continually increasing wages. Even in 1955 the light engineering towns of the Midlands and South-East had acquired a New World gloss. In Coventry, council houses with £60 a week coming in were not uncommon. The prosperity of the "booming" new industries spilled over into other occupations in the "booming" towns, and higher wages had to be paid to unskilled workers on dustcarts and buses.

In spite of the closing down of many coal mines and cotton mills, and in spite of an increasing use of new machinery, there was often not enough labour to satisfy the demands of employers, particularly in prosperous areas of the Midlands and the South-East. Here, in particular, women found it easy to get work—in factories, offices, shops and schools. This often meant that two or three wage packets came into a house.

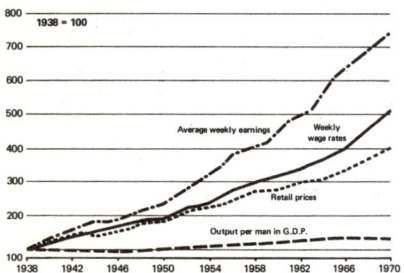

This graph shows the growth of wages, prices and productivity

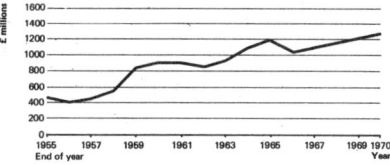

Hire purchase is on the increase. This graph shows the outstanding hire purchase debt

Continental holidays are a feature of the affluent society. The Costa Brava in Spain (seen here) is a very popular place for British holiday-makers. In fact, parts of it have become extremely anglicized, and fish and chips are as easily available as paella

More goods

Higher regular incomes brought a feeling of security which, as Beveridge had said, once belonged only to the aristocracy. Working-class people became property owners on a scale not thought possible in the 1930s. Some bought their own houses [Chapter 10]. More were buying the "consumer durable goods"— a phrase invented by journalists to save them writing down "washing machines, refrigerators, TV sets, gas and electric cookers, central heating systems." These goods and new clothes made of nylon and terylene, new plastic-covered tables, and floor coverings, were products of the scientific-technological revolution of the 1950s. This revolution produced the increasing wealth which provided the money required to pay for the Beveridge social revolution [Chapters 3 and 4], as well as producing the goods for the Marks and Spencer's consumer-goods revolution.

Hire purchase

In the 1930s people who paid for their furniture and other household goods by weekly instalments did so a little shamefacedly. The British thought that there was something "wrong" about the hire purchase system. In post-War Britain this is no longer true. Mr Isaac Wolfson, the Chairman of Great Universal Stores, said in 1958: "The whole nation has taken to buying nearly everything on the instalment plan." During the 1960s, people learned to buy airline tickets and holidays as well as cars and TV sets on hire purchase.

More money means more leisure, and for many, this in turn means more time to spend at the pub

Advertising

Ernest Bevin had talked about the poverty of desire of the British people. In the 1950s and 1960s, the working class could afford, for the first time, to have "great expectations," and the advertising industry grew very rapidly as an increasing number of producers tried to sell their goods to the increasingly affluent British working classes. By 1960 over £1 million per day was being spent on advertising—the second highest figure in the world—in the Press and particularly on commercial television. J. B. Priestley invented a new word—"Admass"—to describe the system of mass advertising; Vance Packard wrote *The Hidden Persuaders* to show that advertising would make people buy things that they did not really want.

Changing workers' world

Perhaps middle-class writers resented the growing affluence of those who had previously been "the lower orders." The affluent workers were more concerned with signing hire purchase forms for a new or second-hand car which allowed them and their families to enjoy a better life—at the weekend or on holiday. In 1961 Ferdynand Zweig, a psychologist, found: "The workers' world was formerly known for its masculinity. The worker had little to do with children or womenfolk. He was a hard-working, hard-swearing, hard-playing man. His manners were often rugged and rough. His voice was often loud, his manner of speaking harsh. Now he has mellowed considerably. The segregation of the sexes is on the decline, he marries earlier, he takes his wife out more frequently, he is more of a home bird."

The Beveridge revolution which provided social security was itself partly responsible for Full Employment. Increased spending by the government on health, housing and education provided jobs for thousands of people. In addition, as John Gunther wrote: " . . . one should mention above all the National Health Service. The fact that a Briton does not ever have to pay more than nominal sums for doctor, dentist or medicine throughout his life has played a role in the current boom and the increase in national purchasing power. This is because the share of the family budget that formerly went to medical care can now be spent otherwise on anything from bacon to hi-fi. The ghastly financial drain caused by severe or prolonged illness is now all but eliminated, which is not only a good thing of itself but releases immense funds for other use."

The poor

However, the classless society did not include the whole country. There were still areas where unemployment was high and wages low. These depressed areas of the 1930s had been named the Development Areas of the 1940s to 1960s; governments tried to persuade firms to expand there—and many did: but never enough to employ all those laid off from the old and declining industries. In these areas, lower family incomes meant that fewer children stayed on at school after the age of fifteen than in the more prosperous South-East.

Nor did everyone, even in the South-East, share the affluence. The sick, the old, people with large families and lower than average wages are among those who still have not shared in the full affluence of Britain.

Critics of the affluent society

Some people, like the Angry Young Men of the 1950s and the Radical Students of the 1960s, thought that the classless society was a mockery. They argued that very little had really changed—the Royal Family, the House of Lords, the Public Schools, Authority—all was the same as it had always been. Few, if any, workers agreed with these intellectual ideas, which seemed to contradict the workers' experience. The worker knew that life was better for him than it had been for his father in the 1930s.

Side by side with affluence is poverty and homelessness. This picture was taken in a homeless accommodation centre run by the London Borough of Camden. It shows three of the seven children of one family. All the cooking is done in the fireplace, since the gas was cut off two years earlier

Chapter thirteen
The decline and rise of the Labour Party 1951–1970

The affluence of the classless society, the result of the social and economic changes that took place after 1945, had its effects on British political life in the 1950s and 1960s.

The Labour Party lost the General Elections of 1951 and 1955 [Chapter 8]. The quarrel between the group led by Aneurin Bevan and the main body of the Party seemed likely to continue after the "dessicated calculating machine," Hugh Gaitskell, became leader of the Party in 1955. In 1956 the Suez crisis reunited the Labour Party while it split the Conservatives [Chapters 14 and 16]. In 1957 Sir Anthony Eden gave up the leadership of the Conservative Party. He was succeeded by Harold Macmillan, who faced yet another crisis and a split in the Party in 1958, when three of his leading Ministers, Mr Peter Thorneycroft, Mr Enoch Powell and Mr Nigel Birch, resigned from the government because they disagreed with Mr Macmillan's policy of increased government spending as a means of lowering the level of unemployment.

Glasgow University students protested against the invasion of Suez in November 1956 – as did students and other people throughout the country

Hugh Gaitskell, on the left, leader of the Labour Party in 1960, talking to Richard Crossman, one of his left-wing opponents. Gaitskell wanted to change the Labour Party constitution by excluding any reference to nationalisation

The 1959 Election

First Suez, then the resignation of Sir Anthony Eden, finally the resignation of leading Ministers. Early in 1959 the public opinion polls, by then a feature of British political life, all predicted that the Labour Party would win the coming General Election. The 1959 Election was the first in which TV played a large part. In 1955 the medium was comparatively new and the politicians were inexperienced. In 1959 each of the Parties took advice from advertising experts on how to conduct a political campaign on TV. People had grown used to seeing "Brand X washes whiter" on commercial TV. In 1959 they saw political parties using all the tricks of the advertisers to try to persuade the voters to support "Party 'Z' which will govern better."

In spite of the opinion polls, in 1959 the Conservative Party won its third successive victory over the Labour Party. No other government had ever succeeded in winning three elections in succession. Equally, no Opposition had ever *lost* three elections in succession. Some members of the Labour Party suggested that the word "Labour" sounded out of date now that "labourers" were becoming "semi-skilled." In 1956 Anthony Crosland, a leading Labour Party economist, suggested that what the Party needed were changes in its policies, particularly with regard to nationalisation. In 1960 Mr Gaitskell suggested that the Party should change its constitution, of which Clause 4 states that the Party will nationalise "all the means of production, distribution and exchange." This general clause, said Mr Gaitskell, was now out of date; the Party did not intend to nationalise much more. Harold Wilson was one of those who opposed this. "It was like telling the Salvation Army that there was no Salvation," he said. But the argument meant that the Labour Party was, once again, divided.

A young CND supporter. She wears the distinctive symbol of the movement

Nuclear disarmament

The decision to spend more on defence had split the Labour Party in 1951 [Chapter 7]. The question of national defence led to bitter argument inside the Party again, in 1960, when the Campaign for Nuclear Disarmament (CND) became prominent.

One of the leaders of the movement was Frank Cousins, a leading trade unionist and member of the Labour Party.

At the Labour Party Conference in Scarborough in 1960 there was a debate on whether Britain should remain a nuclear power or not. Hugh Gaitskell and most of the leaders of the Party argued that Britain had to have nuclear weapons; otherwise, they said, Britain would have no influence over the USA or the Russians. Frank Cousins led the attack against this policy, and succeeded in winning a victory over the official leadership of the Party. Once again the Party was split.

Fortunately for Hugh Gaitskell, the Conservative Party became very unpopular in the winter of 1962, and was itself split over whether or not Britain should join the Common Market [Chapter 15]. In 1962 Mr Gaitskell came out against Britain entering Europe, and the majority of the Party supported him. Unity was restored, and hopes of winning the next election rose, particularly when the Conservative Party's bid to join the Common Market was rejected by General de Gaulle on 14 January 1963. Four days later, on 18 January 1963, Hugh Gaitskell died, and was succeeded by Harold Wilson, who had been the youngest Cabinet Minister in this century when he was appointed President of the Board of Trade in 1947.

Harold Wilson in 1963

Wilson had opposed Hugh Gaitskell's attempts to force the Labour Party to abandon nationalisation, and also his ambitions for Britain to have an independent nuclear weapon. He was fully aware of the changes that had taken place in the affluent 1950s and 1960s. He knew that Mr Macmillan had won the 1959 election largely because he had won the votes of the younger, affluent members of the classless society. Harold Wilson set out to win their support when he spoke at the Party Conference in October 1963: "In Cabinet room and boardroom alike, those with responsibility must be able to speak with the language of the technical age. For the commanding heights of industry to be controlled by men whose only claim is aristocratic connection, or the power of wealth, is as irrelevant to the twentieth century as would be the continued purchase of commissions in the armed forces by lordly amateurs. At the very time when the MCC has abandoned the distinction between amateur and professional, we are content to remain, in science and industry, a nation of gentlemen in a world of players."

1964 Election

This appeal to the new middle class and the promise of

A sit-down protest against nuclear weapons by the Committee of One Hundred

ONE IN THREE VOTED FOR LABOUR

The *Daily Telegraph*'s headline on the Labour election victory of 1964

"efficient, tough government" were among the main reasons for the Labour election victory of 1964. It was not the sort of language that the Party used in 1945, but in 1964 over half the voters had been too young to vote in 1945. They did not remember the 1930s and the Depression. They did not want to be told that the Labour Party had created the Welfare State—they had grown up under Conservative governments which had managed that State very efficiently.

Labour government 1964-70

Many people hoped that the Labour government would be able to run the economy more efficiently than the Conservatives. They hoped that there would be no more inflation, balance of payments deficits and credit squeezes. The Deputy Leader of the Labour Party, George Brown, took charge of a new Ministry, the Department of Economic Affairs, and within a short time produced an impressive number of documents. A National Plan was produced with the co-operation of trade unions, industry and various government departments. It suggested ways in which the

Harold Wilson and George Brown at the Labour Party Conference in 1963

country's national income could be made to grow faster, and the benefits that this would bring to everyone. Representatives of the unions and industry signed a Declaration of Intent, in which they promised to hold down prices and wages so that inflation would be brought to a halt. They also signed an agreement on productivity in which both sides of industry agreed to cooperate in finding more efficient methods of production.

By 1967 the National Plan had been abandoned. The Labour government had found economic facts were stronger than signatures on documents. Wages and prices continued to rise; Britain continued to import more than she exported, and had to borrow increasingly large sums of money from foreign bankers. In July 1966 these bankers insisted that the British government had to attack the twin problems of inflation and balance of payments deficits. The government introduced a credit squeeze which was far harsher than anything that had been brought in by the Conservatives. Even this was unable to solve the balance of payments problem. In November 1967—eighteen years after Sir Stafford Cripps had devalued the pound—Chancellor James Callaghan was forced to devalue the pound again.

As a further measure the government passed an Act which gave the Prices and Incomes Board power over wage negotiations and price increases. This brought the government into conflict with the trade unions. At the 1969 TUC conference, the unions voted for an end to this Act. The government, which owed many millions of pounds to foreign bankers and governments, was unable to agree to do so.

The unions also quarrelled with the Labour government because it tried to bring in a bill limiting the unions' freedom to strike. The bill said that before a union could call a strike, they had to notify the government, which could then order the unions not to strike for twenty-eight days. During this time attempts would be made by the government to solve the dispute. Any union leader who refused to follow this procedure, or any union member going on unofficial strike, would be liable to a fine and a prison sentence of up to three months. Union leaders threatened to withdraw their support from the Labour Party; they also pointed out that the proposed legislation might mean the imprisonment of 20,000 strikers at the Abbey Steelworks in Port Talbot, South Wales, or of 15,000 London dockers who frequently went on strike. The government realised that it could not go ahead with its original proposals. The bill was withdrawn.

The Labour government failed to solve the problem of inflation. It also failed to cary out its promise to reform the trade union movement. These two failures persuaded many people that this government was a failure, although it had succeeded in solving some of the country's major problems. The Industrial Reorganisation Commission was set up to encourage the formation of larger, more efficient companies. The continual attention paid to productivity by the Prices and Incomes Board made more people more conscious of the importance of making the economy more efficient. Exports reached record levels.

The government had also tried to tackle a number of social problems. The Rent Act (1965) had abolished the worst feature of the laissez-faire system set up by the Conservatives; it tried to be fair to landlords while safeguarding the tenants from the danger of eviction. Pensions were increased; a new pension scheme was announced and a "wage-related" system of unemployment and sick benefits was introduced.

The government also accepted the fact that Britain was no longer a world power of the stature of the USA or Russia. The country still spent large sums of money on defence and retained the Polaris submarine as a means of delivering nuclear weapons. But less was spent on defence each year and British overseas commitments were cut.

Between 1964 and 1966, Prime Minister Wilson seemed to have taken over the part played by Mr Macmillan between 1958 and 1960. Newspapers, public opinion polls, popular jokes and cartoons, all illustrated Wilson's hold over the British people. But the credit squeeze of July 1966 and more particularly the devaluation in November 1967 damaged his reputation. Even inside the Labour Party there was talk of "an alternative leader." The resignations of Ministers such as Ray Gunter, Douglas Jay and George Brown revealed divisions inside the government. Public opinion polls and newspapers showed that the country was no longer enchanted with Mr Wilson; and in June 1970 the Conservatives won the General Election.

Cartoonist Cummings, in the *Daily Express* of 11 April 1966, shows Wilson as a chicken sitting on an explosive Easter Egg

Chapter fourteen

The decline of the Conservative Party 1960-66

Loans from foreign countries

In 1960 Mr Macmillan was shown in many cartoons as Mr MacWonder, the man who had reunited the Conservative Party after the Suez crisis and led it to unexpected victory in the 1959 election. He, and his Party, had continued the policies which helped to create the affluent society, in which trade union leaders got annual wage increases for their members. Unfortunately, when wages rise, British goods become more expensive and so more difficult to sell. At the same time, British manufacturers import more raw materials to manufacture the goods which the affluent workers want to buy. So, exports fall while imports rise.

In the 1950s there had been some years when Britain imported more than she exported, and so had a balance of payments deficit. In 1956 the government had had to borrow £201 million

Cartoonist Vicky's view of Macmillan's nightmare: US President Kennedy officiating at the wedding of Britain to Europe. The cartoon appeared on 7 June 1961, and was captioned: "It is becoming clear that the US government wants Britain to join the Common Market"

from the International Monetary Fund (IMF), and £179 million from the United States Export-Import Bank, to cover the difference between what the country spent (on imports) and earned (on exports). Some writers pointed out that a country which had to borrow such large sums could hardly be a Great Power. They pointed out that the people lending this money might stop making loans—which would mean that Britain was bankrupt—or might lend the money only on condition that the British worked harder and spent less (on imports).

In 1961 the government had to borrow £536 million from the International Monetary Fund, nearly twice the amount borrowed in 1956. This time the IMF authorities insisted that the government should take steps to improve Britain's economic position. One of these steps, they insisted, was that Britain should apply to join the European Common Market [Chapter 15]; they also said that the British government should immediately tackle the problem of inflation which, they said, was due to wages increasing too quickly.

TEACHERS UP IN ARMS OVER SALARIES

Headline from the *Daily Telegraph* on the teachers' protest over the freezing of their salaries

1961 freeze

In July 1961 the government announced a "wage freeze." No wage increases would be paid to workers employed by the government, e.g. in the nationalised industries, the Civil Service, or welfare services (such as schools and hospitals). The National Income Commission ("Nicky") was set up, and no wage increases were to be paid by employers in private industry unless the Commission approved. The trade unions refused to accept the government's decisions. Workers in London Docks threatened to strike if they were not given a rise, and the employers gave in. The nationalised Central Electricity Board, instructed by the Minister of Fuel and Power, at first refused to pay a wage increase due to electricians. The electricians' trade union threatened a national strike in the power industry; the Minister intervened, the wage increase was paid and the strike was called off. Nurses and teachers, however, having weaker unions and being unwilling to strike, did not get the pay rises that were due to them in July 1961 [Chapter 17].

Growth of nation's wealth

The national income had been growing steadily since 1945. The national income of other countries had been growing more quickly. Britain's national income grew by only 2 per cent in 1960 and in 1961 it grew by only 1 per cent. If the British national income had grown as rapidly after 1950 as those of Germany and France, then in 1961 Britain would have been better off by about £150 per head of the population. Some of this increased wealth could have gone to the worker in higher wages, some to improving the social services and the armed forces. In 1961, for the first time German, French and Belgian workers were earning more than British workers. They had longer paid holidays and much better social welfare schemes, e.g. for the old and unemployed.

To try to improve Britain's economic performance the Conservative government set up the National Economic Development Council ("Neddy") where trade union leaders, industrialists and government representatives discussed the problems of British industry. This was a major change in the policy of the Conservative government, which had won the 1959 election on the slogan: "Conservative Freedom Works." The application to join the Common Market and the setting up of the Incomes Commission and of the Economic Development Council, mark 1961 as an important year in British history.

At the same time the government wanted to increase the number of unemployed as a way of preventing wages rising. They reduced the amount of work that the government was paying for. British Railways slowed up its modernisation schemes, the Electricity Board built fewer new power stations and local

Vicky's cartoon of 18 July 1961 shows the frequently used slogan "Conservative Freedom Works." The caption reads: "The government sets up the National Economic Development Council"

The first meeting of the National Economic Development Council, 7 March 1962

authorities built fewer new schools. This led to a rise in unemployment in the autumn of 1961. The winter 1962–63 was the worst since 1881 and, as in 1947, bad weather had economic effects. Unemployment rose to over 4 per cent and the popularity of the government fell.

On 13 July 1962 Mr Macmillan sacked over half his Cabinet in the hope that new blood would bring new ideas and win back popular support. A popular song of the time, *Mac the Knife,* was now applied to the Prime Minister. Many Conservatives thought that the Party needed a new leader.

Macmillan's popularity declines

Macmillan became more unpopular during the next year. In November 1962, the Vassall spy trial revealed the incompetence of the nation's security system; in January 1963 de Gaulle's veto on Britain's application to join the Common Market humiliated the government, which had staked its future on succeeding in the negotiations; in March 1963 two journalists were sent to prison because of accusations they had made against the Macmillan government over the Vassall spy trial. Almost all the newspapers attacked the government for this attempt to silence opposition. Throughout May and June 1963 the Press carried stories alleging that the Minister of War, John Profumo, was both a liar and a security risk. His resignation on 5 June 1963 was followed by a Press campaign against the other members of the Macmillan government.

The *Daily Telegraph's* headline on the demand for Cabinet changes

New leader

Early in October 1963, Mr Macmillan went to hospital for a serious operation and on 10 October he announced that he was going to give up the leadership of the Party as soon as a new leader was chosen. Some Conservatives thought that the leadership should go to R. A. Butler, who had been Deputy Leader of the Party since 1955. Some thought that Lord Hailsham (Quintin

CHRISTINE & PROFUMO SEEN

A headline from the *Daily Telegraph* on the scandal concerning Christine Keeler and John Profumo, Minister of War, who resigned his post

Hogg) would bring back respectability to the Party. Others thought that the Party needed a young leader, perhaps Reginald Maudling, the Chancellor of the Exchequer, or Edward Heath, who had led the British delegation in the negotiations over the Common Market. To the surprise of most people, the Conservative Party chose Lord Home, the Foreign Secretary, as leader.

Lord Home gave up his title, won a by-election at Perth, and took his seat in the Commons. He tried to restore the popularity of the government by increasing employment and by promising a more vigorous attack on unemployment in the depressed areas. This increased spending led to a rise in imports—as in 1959-60—and a new balance of payments crisis seemed inevitable.

Elections 1964-70

The 1964 General Election was not the disaster for the Conservatives that many had expected, after the unhappy years 1961-63, for the Labour Party won the election with a majority of only 5. A few more votes in a few constituencies would have given the Conservatives a victory.

In 1965 Sir Alec Douglas Home resigned from the leadership of the Conservative Party and was succeeded by Edward Heath. Both parties were now led by men born in the twentieth century, neither of whom was a member of the aristocracy, both of whom had gone to grammar schools.

Under Mr Heath, the Conservatives lost the 1966 election. This second, successive failure led many Conservatives to write about "many years in the political wilderness." The general view was that Harold Wilson's government would be in office for a long time. By 1970 Harold Wilson's popularity had suffered as did that of Mr Macmillan in 1961–62, and for very much the same reasons. Denied entry into the Common Market (1967), its electoral promises shattered in the anti-inflationary budgets of 1967-69, the Labour Party seemed to be split after the quarrel between the government and the trade union movement over its policies on wages and strikes [Chapters 13 and 17]. In 1966 Wilson had won the sort of reputation that had made Macmillan into Mr Mac-Wonder. In 1970, he seemed as human and fallible as Mr Macmillan was in 1962. In June 1970 Mr Heath led the Conservative Party to victory in the election.

Lord Home after making a speech on foreign affairs at the Conservative Party Conference in Blackpool, 1963

Chapter fifteen
The Common Market

When the War ended in 1945, Britain was one of the few countries in Western Europe that had not been a battlefield. Most other countries had been occupied by the Germans, who had later been driven back by native resistance movements and Allied invasions. Millions of Europeans suffered in 1940-41 as the Germans advanced; millions of others suffered in 1944-45 as the Allies drove the Germans out.

European unity

In 1970 both the Labour and Conservative governments said they were willing to take Britain into Europe, provided that the Six made adequate concessions. Both parties have been influenced by British public opinion, which appears to be less eager to enter Europe in 1970 than in 1962 or 1966. The memory of the most destructive war in history was one of the main reasons for the growth of the idea of a United Europe. In 1948 the leaders of Germany (Dr Adenauer), Italy (de Gasperi) and France (Robert Schumann) spoke for the majority of Europeans when they pointed out how stupid it was that wars between European states should lead to the destruction of Europe; they proposed that European nations should try to form some sort of a United States of Europe in which there would be no war.

Europe had once been the centre of the world; the Greeks and Romans had left a heritage of civilisation which other parts of

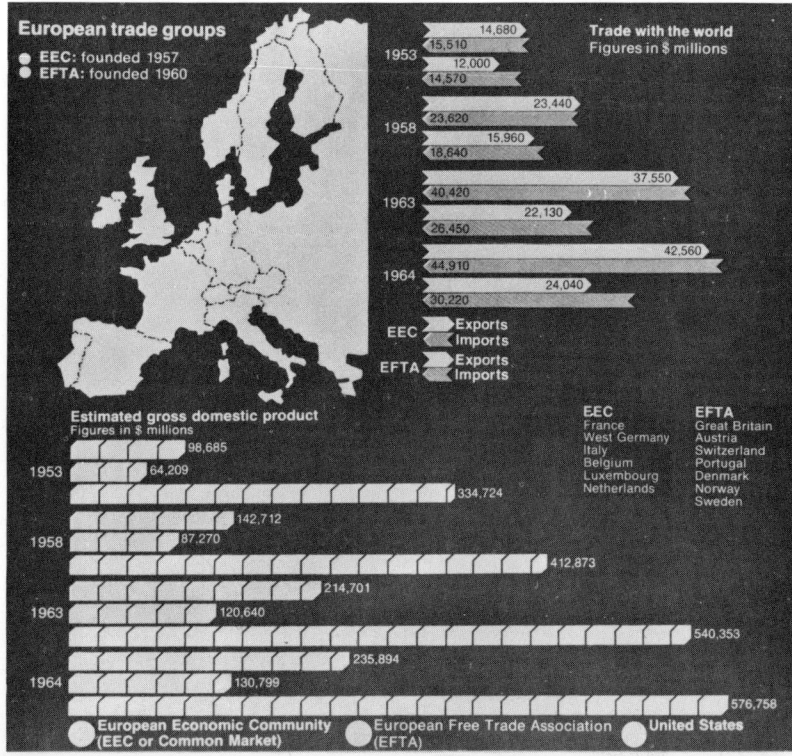

European trade groups showing the European Economic Community, formed by the Six to create a single market between them; and the European Free Trade Area, established by Britain

the world have since adopted; from Europe there had grown Spanish, French, Dutch and British Empires, each of them, in their time, huge and powerful. By 1945 it was obvious to most Europeans that the centre of world power had passed away from Europe. America and Russia were now so powerful that no single European power would ever again have the influence which France or Britain had had in the past.

Another reason for uniting Europe was economic. In the nineteenth century fairly small businesses, often family-owned, had been big enough to develop the new industries. Machinery was relatively cheap and small, compared to the machinery and equipment in the new industries of the twentieth century. This machinery was expensive, and these industries were soon dominated by a few, very large, firms. In the future machinery and industry would become even more complicated and expensive. Some firms would be so large that they would have to be controlled by the government (e.g. the British Atomic Energy Authority). Some industrial ventures would be so costly that two or more governments would have to share the cost (e.g. the French and British governments have co-operated in developing the *Concorde*). Russia and America, both very large countries with big populations, can stand on their own in the new technological world; it is clear that smaller countries cannot afford to do so.

Progress towards unity

In 1948 European countries receiving Marshall Aid set up the Organisation for European Economic Co-operation. Some people hoped that from this economic co-operation governments might develop closer political links. In 1949 NATO was established, and some people hoped that military necessity might be the basis on which a United Europe would be built. In 1949 the

The signing of the Rome Treaties, which set up the Common Market and Euratom on 25 March 1957. The signatories were from left to right: P. H. Spaak and J. Ch. Snoy et d'Oppuers (Belgium), C. Pineau and M. Fauro (France), K. Adenauer and W. Hallstein (Germany), A. Segni and C. Martino (Italy), J. Bech and L. Schaus (Luxembourg), J. Luns and J. Linthorst Homan (Netherlands)

General de Gaulle and Harold Macmillan after a meeting to discuss Britain's entry into the Common Market in 1962

Council for Europe held its first meeting at Strasbourg; here members of the Parliaments of all the Western European countries met regularly to discuss matters of common interest, such as trade development and international relations, and it was hoped that this "European Parliament" might be the first stage on the road to a United Europe.

For the first two or three years after the War, Europe waited for Britain to give a lead towards uniting Europe. Mr Churchill, who became Chairman of an all-party committee to launch the United Europe campaign, spoke of the common heritage of spiritual values which all European countries had received from Rome and Greece; some Labour politicians saw a United Europe as a zone of sanity between Moscow and Washington. But the British were not really European-minded. Winston Churchill said "To take a homely test, we may just as well see what the girl looks like before we marry her."

Economic unity

In 1949 Robert Schumann and Jean Monnet of France ignored Britain's lack of interest and persuaded the governments of France, West Germany, Italy, Belgium, Holland and Luxembourg to hand over their coal and steel industries to the European Coal and Steel Community. This organisation was to be independent of the governments and would run the coal and steel industries of all six countries as one industry. Britain was invited to take part in the discussions which led to the formation of this Community, but Ernest Bevin refused to have anything to do with them, and when the Conservatives came to power in 1951 they only sent an observer to report on the discussions.

The Coal and Steel Community was a great success. The output of the two industries increased by over 25 per cent and contributed to the speedy recovery of Europe from the effects of the War. It also proved that it was possible for "the Six" to give up some power (over their industries) to an independent organisation, and to benefit from this. In 1955 representatives of the Six governments met at Messina, Italy, to discuss the possibility of creating a new organisation which would control each country's economic, social, financial and political policy. Britain was invited to attend this meeting. As journalist Norah Beloff wrote: "Neither Macmillan nor anyone else in the Eden Government saw any reason to get excited over the advance at Messina . . . The only important thing was that the Six were now talking about trade; the Board of Trade, it was felt, should find out what was happening . . . .

Britain sent an official from the Board of Trade, Mr Bretherton . . . He was told to make the Europeans understand that if they were again up to their supranational tricks they could not expect Whitehall to take them seriously.

In November, at a meeting presided over by Spaak, Bretherton outlined the reasons for Britain's apprehension, her opposition to any arrangement which might collide with her Commonwealth commitment and her insistence that the Community must remain inside the OEEC framework. The continentals listened and at the end of the meeting everybody shook hands and left on friendly terms. There was no drama. Only that happened to be the last time British officials were invited to any Brussels meetings. Mr Bretherton packed his bags and went home. The Committee quietly began to draft their report which was to be the basis of the subsequent Rome Treaty, and Britain had nothing more to do with negotiating the Common Market..."

The European Economic Community

The Six agreed to create a European Economic Community, to lower and finally abolish all tariffs between them so that eventually the Six would be one single market. They also agreed to impose a tariff on all goods coming into the Community from outside.

Britain was interested in some of these ideas. As a major exporting country, she wanted to see tariffs lowered, since lower tariffs lead to lower prices, and make it easier to sell British goods. But Britain is also a major importing country, particularly of food, which she imports, without any tariff, from Australia, Canada and New Zealand. If Britain became a member of the Six, she would have to put a tariff on such imports so that the French and German farmers could sell their dearer food in Britain. This was one reason why Britain withdrew from the Messina Conference in 1955.

Cartoonist Cummings' view of General de Gaulle's attitude to the British in general and Mr Heath in particular over the Common Market

"Ha, Mr. Heath! You're just De Gaulle's spaniel!"

The European Economic Community was established by the Treaty of Rome signed on 25 March 1957 and came into operation on 1 January 1958.

Britain was interested in the idea of a wider Free Trade Area, and throughout 1956 and 1957 Mr Maudling led a British team in negotiations with the Six to try to persuade them to accept a system by which European countries cut tariffs on trade between one another, but remained free to do what they wanted about tariffs on goods from outside Europe. Britain would have stood to gain from this. Her cars and other manufactured goods would have gone tariff-free into Europe while she continued to import cheaper Commonwealth food. The French and the Germans felt that there was no profit in this for them. They also pointed out that the Community was not merely an economic undertaking. It was also a stage along the road to a United Europe. If Britain wanted to join a United Europe she would have to join it wholeheartedly, and not try to keep her ties with the Commonwealth.

The European Free Trade Area

After failing to impose her views on the Six, Britain established the European Free Trade Area as a second best to the EEC. In EFTA, each country is allowed to keep or reject tariffs on goods from non-EFTA countries, while tariffs on goods coming from other EFTA partners are to be abolished. EFTA countries have a population of about 100 million, and apart from Britain their national income per head of population is very much lower than that of the countries in EEC which, in spite of the tariffs against British goods, was a larger market for British products in 1969.

When the British government borrowed money from the IMF in 1961, it is thought that one of the secret conditions attached to the loan was that Britain had to apply to join the EEC. This had not been discussed in the 1959 election campaign. Indeed, many British people seemed to think that the Europeans deserved to fail if they rejected Britain's advice on free trade. In August 1961 Sir Derek Walker Smith, a Conservative Member of Parliament, attacked his government's sudden decision to apply for entry, saying "The sovereignty of Parliament and the rule of Law are the twin pillars of our Constitution and way of life. For the Six, Parliament has its roots less deep." Mr Shinwell spoke for many of his Labour Party colleagues when he said: "I wonder what this place (Parliament) will be like during the next ten years (if Britain joined EEC). There will not be 630 honourable members. There will be no need for more than 150 or so. It will be like a parish council."

This "fear of the foreigner" was deeper in 1961 than in 1970. The Labour Party, which had always spoken about "the brotherhood of man," found unity in 1962 behind Hugh Gaitskell when he spoke about the danger of turning one's back on "a thousand years of history." On the other hand the Conservative Party was bitterly divided on Mr Macmillan's decision to apply for entry.

In June 1967 de Gaulle was visited at Versailles by the British Prime Minister Wilson, for yet more discussions on entry into the Common Market

...TO BRITAIN'S BID TO JOIN THE COMMON MARKET...
...TO KENNEDY'S NASSAU OFFER OF THE POLARIS...

NON!

de Gaulle blocks the way

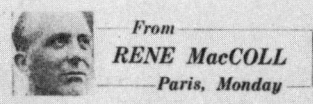

From RENE MacCOLL —Paris, Monday—

PRESIDENT DE GAULLE tonight brusquely denied Britain's entry into the Common Market—unless Britain is prepared to jettison all the major reservations she has had so far about the terms of membership. De Gaulle also turned down President Kennedy's offer of the Polaris missile

A typical newspaper headline on de Gaulle's blocking attitude. This one appeared in the *Daily Express* on 15 January 1963

In July 1962 President Kennedy had suggested that the EEC should try to create a world-wide free trade system. To the Six this seemed like an attempt to re-open the debate with the British which, they thought, they had finished in 1957. Britain was closely linked with the USA. When Britain applied to join EEC, some Europeans, notably de Gaulle, were afraid that this would enable the American government to gain influence in EEC. In December 1962 Macmillan met President Kennedy at Nassau and they agreed that America should supply Polaris missiles to Britain. The Americans had refused to supply the French or Germans with such weapons. This was an indication of the "special relationship" between Britain and America, of which both governments spoke and which the French in particular resented.

In January 1963 General de Gaulle vetoed Britain's application to join EEC.

The immediate effect of this humiliation was the collapse of the Conservative Party's economic policies, which had been based on the assumption that Britain would succeed in joining the Community.

Neither Party raised the issue at the 1964 election but leading members of the Labour government were in favour of joining EEC. Mr Heath tried to persuade the government to make a fresh application and to accept whatever terms the Six offered. The Labour government was unwilling to repeat the humiliation of 1963 and Harold Wilson and George Brown made journeys to each of the capitals of the Six to sound out opinion before making a fresh application. When they thought that they had got some support in each of the six countries they applied to join EEC. Once again, however, the General said "No." General de Gaulle's resignation in 1968 led to a fresh examination by both the British and the Europeans of the problem of Britain's joining the EEC, although the Heath government and public opinion seem less eager to join in 1970 than in 1962 and 1966.

Chapter sixteen
The British Empire—part 2: Africa

Reasons for Britain's decline

Britain's victories in two World Wars had been won at a great cost. She was much poorer in 1945 than she had been in 1939 whilst the United States had become economically stronger than Britain, and both the USA and Russia were militarily stronger. After 1945 Britain was no longer the "workshop of the world;" she had to accept Marshall Aid to help her to recover from the War. The country which had once financed the industrial development of the world had to borrow money in 1957 and 1961 and after 1964, because she was unable to export enough to pay for her imports.

After 1949 Britain's Foreign Secretary sat as one among equals with other members of NATO, no longer able to force governments to do what he wanted, no longer the centre of the world's attention as Neville Chamberlain had been.

Signs of decline of British power

The granting of independence to India and Pakistan, the humiliation of Abadan, and the withdrawal from the Suez Canal bases, were only three of the many signs that Britain's power was less than it had been. In March 1956, General John Glubb—Glubb Pasha, founder of the Arab Legion and one of a long line of British supporters of Arab nationalism—was dismissed from his post and expelled from the country by young King Hussein of Jordan. To many this seemed the final insult. British patriotism wanted a chance to assert itself.

General John Glubb, who founded the Arab Legion, was expelled from Jordan in 1956

Neville Chamberlain speaking at Heston Airport on 30 September 1938, when he returned from Munich after talks with Hitler. He was sure that Hitler wanted peace – but in 1939 war between Britain and Germany broke out. At the end of this War, Britain was in dire financial straits and was never again the Great Power she had been before the War

Suez Crisis, 1956

In the middle of 1952 an Army revolt had ended the corrupt rule of King Farouk of Egypt. Led by Colonel Nasser, a new Egyptian government started to tackle the problem of poverty by a policy of social and land reform. One of Nasser's main projects was the High Dam at Aswan which was to provide hydro-electric power for the development of industry, and water to irrigate large areas of desert. Egypt had to ask foreign countries for the money, materials and technicians to build this Dam. America, Britain and Russia were among those who promised help.

In 1955 Egypt was at war with Israel, and had bought weapons from Communist Czechoslovakia. The American Secretary of State, John Foster Dulles, was afraid that Egypt would go Communist. This suspicion was increased by Nasser's continued friendship with Russia. The Americans thought that he was using this Russian link to get more aid from the USA. On 19 July 1956 Dulles announced that the US government would not finance the building of the High Dam, and on the next day the British followed suit.

On 26 July 1956 Nasser announced that his government was going to nationalise the Suez Canal Company and would use the income from the Canal to pay for the building of the Dam. The Suez Canal Company was owned largely by French and British shareholders, but the Company was registered in Egypt and the Canal ran through Egyptian territory. The move was provocative, although Nasser had as much right to nationalise this Company as the British government had to nationalise the coal

The Aswan Dam under construction

Gamal Abdul Nasser, who started revitalising Egypt after his take over from King Farouk in 1952. He did much to improve the conditions of the poor in Egypt. He was also a leading figure in Arab Nationalism

industry. He promised to pay the shareholders a compensation based on the value of their shares before nationalisation.

The British Press, politicians and public were not interested in the legality of his claim. For many years they had been taught, and believed that the Canal was the "lifeline of the British Empire." Even though the rights of the Canal Company were due to expire in 1968 (one hundred years after its formation), the British still thought of the Canal as theirs even though since 1948 they had given in to Egyptian pressure, and refused to allow ships going to or from Israeli ports to go through the Canal.

Nasser rejected a proposal from the US and other countries that the Canal should be placed under the control of an International Suez Canal Company. The British Press demanded tough action from the British government. The French government was willing to take action against Nasser because he supported the Algerian rebels in their struggle for independence from France.

The Israeli government was frightened that if Nasser succeeded in defying the "white man's world" he might unite the Arab world for a war against Israel. There had been border skirmishes between the two countries since 1948; in 1955 this blew up into a small war when Israeli forces invaded the Gaza peninsula, blew up an Egyptian army post and killed thirty-seven Egyptian soldiers.

There are conflicting accounts of what happened in the summer of 1956. What seems certain is that in October 1956, leaders of the British, French and Israeli governments met at Sèvres, in France, and agreed to invade Egypt. On 29 October 1956 Israel attacked; in six days they had defeated the Egyptian army and reached the Gulf of Akaba. On 30 October, British and French troops landed at Port Said after an air and sea bombardment.

A letter in the *Daily Telegraph* said: "How good it is to hear the British Lion's roar." The *Sunday Express* called it: "The proudest week we have known for years." Not everyone agreed.

N SUEZ USER TIONS ACCEPT

The *Daily Telegraph*'s headline on the nationalisation of the Suez Canal, 26 July 1956

In public houses, shops, factories and schools all over England, there was bitter and fierce argument. People who opposed the government's policy were called traitors. The *Observer* wrote about the government's "folly and crookedness."

Britain had invaded Egypt in 1882 and none of the other powers had been able to do anything to stop her. In 1956, one day after the troops had landed, the government was forced to halt the advance down the Canal. (Lord) Attlee had been right about Abadan [Chapter 7]. The decision to invade Egypt had split the country, roused the Opposition, angered the Americans and brought threats of a rocket attack from the Russians. The Americans threatened to withdraw financial support from the British government. At the United Nations the invasion was condemned almost unanimously—and Britain had to withdraw her troops to allow a United Nations Force to move in to try to keep peace between Israel and Egypt.

The Egyptians had sunk several ships in the Canal so that even if the British had recaptured it, they would have found it difficult to use. The Canal was not opened again until 1958. The "lifeline of the Empire" was temporarily severed. The Prime Minister, Sir Anthony Eden, went to Jamaica for a holiday and announced his resignation from the leadership of the Conservative Party.

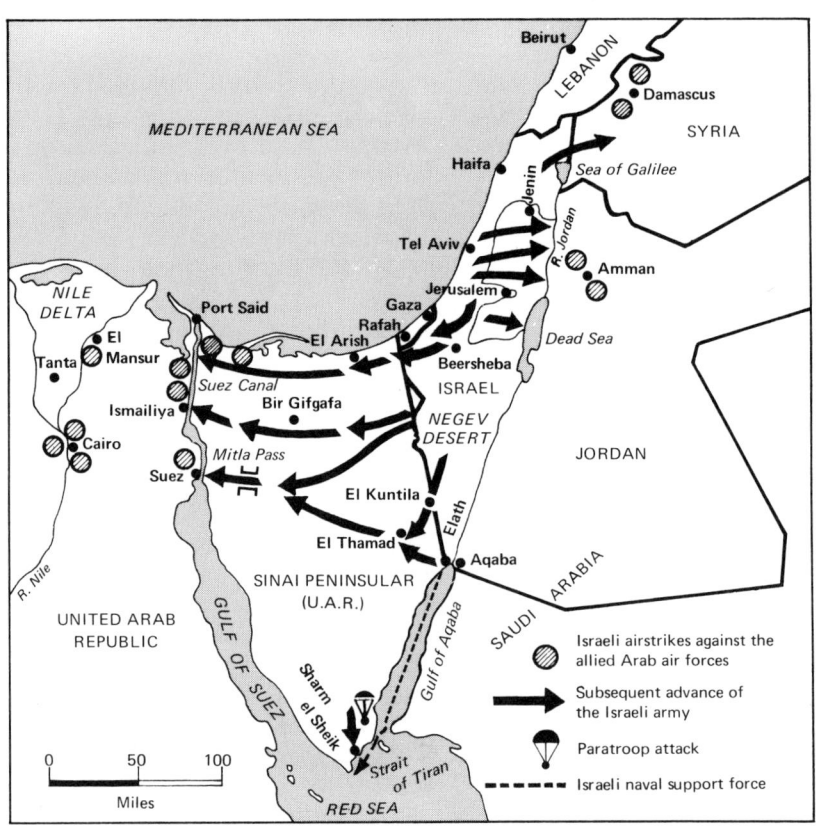

This map shows fighting in the June War between Egypt and Israel in 1967

United Nations troops patrolling the main streets in Gaza after the appointment of a new governor by Nasser

African countries become independent

At the end of the nineteenth century, Africa was divided between European powers who had paid no attention to the wishes of the native tribes. Nigeria, for example, has within its border 50 million people speaking 248 languages. Large tribes like the Hausas (14 million), the Yoruba (13 million), and Ibos (8 million), have their own cultures and, by European standards, are separate nations as the civil war (1968–70) showed.

By 1945 Britain was no longer strong enough to defend a large Empire, and Russia and America encouraged nationalist movements. During the War many black Africans had met Europeans in the Forces, and had discovered that not all Englishmen believed in the idea of Empire. Some Africans had gone to Western universities and learned Western ideas about freedom, justice and democracy. It is not surprising that in the early 1950s there were uprisings against European power in Africa.

Mr Churchill had said: "I have not become the King's First Minister to preside over the liquidation of the British Empire." But it was Conservative Ministers who made the agreement with Egypt for the evacuation of British troops from the Canal Zone and a Conservative government which released Kwame N'krumah from gaol in the Gold Coast to lead his Party after a victory in the General Election and to independence in 1957. Malaya (1957), the Sudan (1956), Cyprus (1959), Nigeria (1960), Tanganyika and Zanzibar (1960), Sierra Leone (1961) and Kenya (1963), all became independent during the rule of the Conservative Party in Britain.

Rhodesia

In 1963 the Central African Federation of Rhodesia, Nyasaland and Zambia was broken up, and Zambia and Malawi (Nyasaland) became independent countries ruled over by African politicians. Southern Rhodesia, ruled by the representatives of the white minority, asked for independence. The Conservative government refused this request until there were signs that the African majority was being educated and sharing in the government of their country.

In 1964, when the Labour government came to power in Britain, Ian Smith, leader of the United Front Party in Southern Rhodesia, announced that he would take the country to independence with or without Britain's permission. Throughout 1965 negotiaions between the two countries went on, and in December 1966 it seemed that talks between Mr Wilson and Mr Smith on board *HMS Tiger* had brought a solution. When Mr Smith returned to Southern Rhodesia, he said that the terms offered by Mr Wilson were not acceptable; and that plans for Southern Rhodesian independence would go ahead. Attempts by Britain and, later, the United Nations, to crush this rebellion, by stopping all trade with Southern Rhodesia, failed.

British influence in the 1960s

Before 1939 Britain's Foreign Ministers had been at the centre of world affairs. In October 1962, the Russian attempt to build rocket bases on Cuba almost led to a nuclear war between Russia and America. Neither Mr Kruschev of Russia, nor President Kennedy of America, was influenced by the opinion of the British government. Both knew that the British depended on American aid in economic and defence matters. Since 1964 the British government has sent envoys to Hanoi and to Washington to try to bring peace to Vietnam. Neither the Communist rulers in Hanoi, nor the various Presidents in Washington, appear to have been influenced by British pressure. Perhaps most revealing of all was Britain's failure to bring to an end a civil war inside Nigeria, where the Ibos declared their independence in 1968.

Britain is still a powerful industrial country and one of the wealthiest in the world. But compared with Russia and America, Britain is in a second league, whereas in the nineteenth century she was often top of the first league. Older people find this difficult to understand and more difficult to accept, but events in Africa and Asia are the best evidence of the true position of twentieth century Britain.

Ian Smith at 10 Downing Street in 1965. So far all attempts to overthrow the illegal regime set up by Mr Smith have failed

Chapter seventeen
The trade unions

A great change has taken place in Britain in the last thirty years in the power of the trade union movement. The Chamberlain government which declared war on Germany in September 1939 did not consult the leaders of the trade union movement about the contribution that they or their members might make towards the war effort. Chamberlain had been a member of the Cabinet in 1926 when the General Strike seemed, to some members of the Cabinet, like the beginnings of a Workers' Revolt. In 1939 Chamberlain still regarded the union movement as revolutionary.

Unions in wartime

Churchill became Prime Minister in 1940. He had been the most active anti-union member of the 1926 Cabinet. But in 1940 he recognised the importance of getting working-class support if Britain was going to win the War. He immediately invited Ernest Bevin, who was not then even a Member of Parliament, to become Minister of Labour. His Ministry persuaded the unions to accept direction of labour. Some industries and trades were classified as "essential": no worker was allowed to leave an "essential" occupation; employers in such industries could recruit extra labour only through the local offices of the Ministry of Labour.

The unions gave up many of their privileges; they allowed unskilled workers to do work that had previously been done only by skilled men, which led to an increased output of war material. Union members were active in arbitration councils set up to solve industrial disputes, and in the countless advisory and productivity councils set up by the government.

In 1942 when the Beveridge Report was published, the Coalition government was lukewarm towards it, and the Labour

George Woodcock addressing a conference of the Trades Union Congress especially convened to discuss an incomes policy

Ministers in that government, particularly Herbert Morrison, argued that it was too idealistic. But the Trade Union Congress (TUC), representing the trade union movement, supported Beveridge's ideas. Beveridge acknowledged his debt to the union movement when he called the unions "the Godfathers of the Beveridge Report."

The Report, and the publication of the government's White Paper on Full Employment (1944), caused the TUC to set out its own ideas in an Interim Report on Post-War Reconstruction (1944). It expressed the hope that the post-War governments would ensure that there would be no more depressions like those of the years after the First World War. The TUC recognised that one problem resulting from full employment would be wage-inflation. Almost everyone would have a job. If an employer wanted to recruit extra labour he would have to offer higher wages to attract men from their existing place of work. Their current employer might not want to lose his workers, so he would make an even higher offer. In this situation trade unions would be able to use the scarcity of labour as a strong bargaining counter in their negotiations with the employers and would be able to push up wage rates.

Unions and wages policy, 1945-60

The TUC Report (1944) promised that if the government used its powers to guarantee full employment, and to stop prices and profits from rising, the trade unions would not use their power to drive up wages. This was the first of many statements on a "wages policy." The unions refused to give up their right to bargain with employers on behalf of their members. They refused

Vicky's cartoon of 22 November 1961 shows Prime Minister Macmillan with the Chancellor, Selwyn Lloyd, whose pay pause collapsed in the face of union pressure

George Woodcock (right) looks on after the signing of a Joint Statement of Intent on Productivity, Prices and Incomes, signed by Maurice Laing, for the British Employers, the Minister George Brown, and Lord Collison for the TUC

to accept the need for government interference in wage negotiations. One of the most powerful trade union leaders in 1945 was Arthur Deakin, Secretary of the Transport and General Workers Union who said, of a planned wages policy: "We will have none of that."

The victory of the Labour Party in 1945 was welcomed by the trade union movement. This was their government. In 1946 Arthur Deakin could boast: "We have an open door in relation to all State departments." The social revolution of 1945-48 was their revolution. Full employment was at last a reality and the unions, as they had promised in 1944, did not abuse their powers. In 1948, Sir Stafford Cripps proposed a period of "wage freeze" when the unions would not ask for any wage increases. This, it was hoped, would allow British export prices to stay steady and make the job of selling exports easier. This freeze was maintained throughout 1948 and 1949. Unfortunately, [Chapter 7], the Korean War led to an increase in the price of imported food and raw material. The union leaders called off the wage freeze in 1950 because the combination of stable wages and rising prices had led to a fall in the standard of living of their members.

Changing political attitudes

In 1951, when the Conservative government came to power, a minority of trade unionists wanted to use the power of the movement as a weapon against this government.

But by now many trade union leaders had become less politically conscious. They had seen that nationalisation was not the cure-all for the workers' problems. Industrial relations in the nationalised coal industry were less bitter than they had been in the 1920s, but strikes were frequent. Workers on British Railways

'Down, dammit, down'

[*Guardian*, Apr. 20th, 1965]

Papas' cartoon of 20 April 1965 shows George Brown trying hard to control incomes while prices rise

had as little say in management decisions as in the days of private enterprise. Meanwhile, full employment and the social security of the Welfare State provided the working man with a high standard of living In the opinion of many union members there seemed little that political activity could do, especially since the new Conservative government promised to continue the employment and welfare policies of its Labour predecessor.

After twelve years of Conservative government, George Woodcock, the General Secretary of the TUC, said: "We created the Labour Party to get what we wanted. Now we've got it, we don't need it in the same way. The Labour Party's job is to get votes. Our job is to get wages." Throughout the affluent 1950s the unions succeeded in doing their job and the standard of living of their members rose.

Hostility towards the unions

This increasing affluence was not welcomed by everyone. White-collared workers resented the fact that by 1955, for example, the average manual worker's wage was equal to that of the average bank clerk aged twenty-eight, and was considerably ahead of the local government clerk of the same age [Chapter 11]. Bank clerks, local government clerks, teachers and other members of the middle classes recalled days "before the War."

Since the trade unions had been a main factor in the growth of working class prosperity and since higher wages and costs were a cause of the fall in the living standards of the older middle classes, it is not surprising that there was, in the 1950s, a good deal of resentment against the trade union movement. Some of this resentment led people to demand strong government action against workers who went on strike—although all too often these strikes were "unofficial" and were not called by the union leaders.

In July 1961 Mr Selwyn Lloyd imposed a pay pause, announcing that for an indefinite time the government would not allow any wage or salary increases. This singled out wages and salaries as the causes of inflation, an opinion not universally held; it ignored, for instance, the rises in profits and prices, which the TUC Report of 1944 considered to be as important as wage rates.

Employees in the public service suffered most during this period, as their employer, the government, could ensure that the pay pause was observed in their case. Other workers suffered in inverse ratio to the strength of their union. The electricians challenged the government when their union was awarded a pay increase which the Central Electricity Board, under the direction of the Minister of Fuel and Power, threatened not to honour. The union went ahead with plans for a strike of electricians in the power industry. At the last minute the Minister intervened, agreed to pay the increased wage, and the strike was called off. Nurses, having only a weak union and being unwilling to use the threat of a strike, were less fortunate.

Unions for middle-class workers

The growth of new industries has led to an increased use of machinery, automated plant and computer systems. Skilled workmen are required to build and operate this new equipment. To organise the new labour force, new unions have come into being, and some old ones have been enlarged. The Association of Scientific, Technical and Managerial Staffs, and the Draughtsmen's and Allied Technicians' Association, recruit highly qualified and scarce white-collared workers. These men have no bitter memories of the 1930s; they welcome talk about increased productivity since they profit from technological advances.

They were not the first unions for white-collared workers in Britain. Civil Servants, journalists, Post Office workers, clerks and teachers had all formed unions before 1914. After 1945 there was an increase in the membership of many of these older, "respectable" unions, and in the late 1950s and in the 1960s they became increasingly militant. Salaried people believed that union activity was a main cause of the improved status of the wage-earner. They hoped, perhaps, that similar activity on their part might lead to similar improvement in their status, and so their unions became involved in traditional trade union activity. Teachers went on strike. Bank clerks picketed strike-bound banks.

These campaigns have succeeded. Nurses have won a 40-hour working week, with extra pay for any hours worked above this. Teachers no longer have to do lunch duties. Bank clerks have won a five-day week, and banks no longer open on Saturdays.

Teachers on strike in Ipswich march through the streets demanding better pay and conditions

As Minister of Health in 1961, Enoch Powell refused to allow nurses to receive a wage award. Fortunately for the Health Service, there was a vast influx of coloured immigrants who worked in hospitals and saved the situation

The TUC

The General Council of the TUC has been given increased powers by individual unions. They have agreed not to call a strike until they have notified the General Council, which uses its influence to try to settle the dispute, so that members of other unions are not thrown out of work. In 1965 the individual unions agreed to notify the General Council before applying for a wage increase. The General Council examines the union's claim for an increase and either supports the claim or advises the union not to go ahead with it.

In 1969 the Labour government published a White Paper called *In Place of Strife,* intended to be the basis of new legislation about trade unions. The White Paper suggested that no strike should be called until the union concerned had given 28 days notice of its intention to strike. During this "cooling-off" period a new Commission on Industrial Relations would try to settle the dispute. If the Commission failed, then the strike could go ahead. The White Paper suggested that any union, or any group of workers acting without the union's permission, which called a strike without following this procedure, would be liable to imprisonment and a fine.

This brought the TUC and the government into conflict. After several months of negotiation the government agreed to drop the idea of an Act based on the White Paper, while the TUC agreed to set up its own Committee to try to prevent strikes taking place. While the TUC had a number of successes in 1969, it still failed to prevent a strike, which lasted eight weeks, at the Port Talbot steelworks (South Wales), as well as numerous strikes in the motor-car industry.

STEEL STRIKE THREATENS CAR FIRMS

Race to get stocks from Continent

This *Daily Telegraph* **headline on a 1969 steel strike is sadly typical**

Chapter eighteen
Immigration and emigration

In his autobiography, Sir Oswald Mosley recalls a 1959 by-election in North Kensington, London. The people "were all enjoying full employment and the high and increasing wages of the affluent society. Most of them had either personal or childhood memories of unemployment, the misery and mass starvation of the thirties; they would think twice before upsetting the apple-cart of the affluent society. A glance at the television set and car (both) on hire purchase, and indignation would cool at the thought of possibly losing them through some big change." He thought that the affluent society was the main reason for his poor showing at the election. Bessie Braddock, a leading Labour MP, thought that the affluent society was the main reason why the Labour Party did so badly in the 1959 General Election. She said: "Right now the basic insecurity the worker feels is this; they are haunted by the spectre of the van driving up to the door to take away the TV set."

Immigrant workers

Full employment and high wages for the majority of workers meant that it was difficult to find enough workers to take less well paid, unpleasant or dirty jobs. This was particularly true in the South-East and the Midlands. Many employers had set up agencies in Malta and Cyprus to recruit workers there, and in the early 1950s about 20,000 coloured immigrant workers and their families arrived each year from Asia, Africa or the West Indies.

West Indians arriving at Victoria Station, London. They have come in the belief that they will be happier and better paid than in their native islands. A few manage to make this dream come true; but many are disillusioned by problems of housing and employment

Emigrants

In the 1950s and 1960s many people in Britain believed that they were paying higher taxes than people in other countries. In fact, the British government collects less taxes than governments in most of the other leading industrial countries, including the USA. What is true is that the British pay a high level of direct tax, on incomes, profits and dividends. Most other countries collect the greater part of their taxes by indirect taxation. People are very often not aware of the amount they are paying in indirect tax (on petrol, on clothes) but they do know how much they pay each week or month in income tax. Many people emigrated from Britain to escape from this high level of direct taxation and went to the USA, Australia, Canada or New Zealand.

Many others emigrated because they were being paid too small a wage in Britain. Teachers, nurses and other professional workers saw that their standard of living was not rising as rapidly as that of the strongly unionised workers. They emigrated in search of higher wages.

One of the effects of this emigration was to create a shortage of doctors and nurses which coloured immigrants were willing to fill. They left their own countries, where they were badly needed, to come to Britain, where they hoped to gain wider experience while earning money.

Britain's first coloured headmistress was appointed in February 1969. She is a Jamaican, Mrs Yvonne Connolly, seen here with some of her pupils in Islington, London

Race riots in Notting Hill, London, caused great tension

Coloured immigrants

During the War many coloured soldiers in the Indian, Jamaican or Nigerian forces came to Britain; some stayed after the War and liked the country where they had a job with good wages, and where there were social services to look after them when they were sick or unemployed. They contrasted this with conditions in their own countries, where it was difficult to find work, where wages were low, and poverty and ill-health were common. Not surprisingly, when they wrote letters home, their comments on life in Britain led others to emigrate, like the British emigrants, in search of higher wages.

Up to 1959 about 20,000 coloured immigrants arrived each year. In 1960 the boom which had won Mr Macmillan the 1959 election attracted 58,000 immigrants; and in 1961 over 136,000 arrived. By 1964 over one million coloured immigrants had arrived in Britain. Although this is a small proportion of the British population, the coloured immigrants were not evenly spread over the country. They tended to live in certain areas, such as the Midlands, the South-East, and the West Riding of Yorkshire. These were the areas where there were jobs, and where they found friends among the other immigrants.

In general they went into the lower-paid jobs. Most of them were unskilled workers with little or no previous industrial training or experience. The few who were better qualified found it difficult to persuade employers to give them a job equal to their qualifications or ability. Some employers (e.g. the banks, insurance companies and many retailing firms) were unwilling to employ coloured workers. Having a lower wage they were forced to rent or buy poorer quality housing.

Sir Oswald Mosley claimed that the housing shortage was a major cause of racial tension in North Kensington in 1958 and 1959: "The injury to our people in importing to already disgracefully over-crowded areas a large population with a different way of life would have been just as grave if it had been Eskimos instead of Negroes. If you are living in badly overcrowded conditions, it irritates you to have a lot more people dumped on top of you."

In August 1958 "race riots" broke out in North Kensington, confined generally to a small number of trouble-seeking toughs, often the sort who in the late 1960s took to "football rioting" instead. In August 1958 it was not safe for coloured people to go on to the streets in North Kensington, where racist groups found the coloured immigrant a substitute for the Jew whom they used to attack in the 1930s.

The shortage of good houses was one reason why some people resented the influx of large numbers of coloured immigrants. The Welfare State had still not provided enough houses; nor had it done enough for education. When the coloured children went to the nearest school they often made up the majority of a class. Since many of them knew little or no English, the teachers had

to spend more time with them than with the children of English parents. This problem could have been tackled if there had been enough teachers to divide the coloured children up into smaller classes, where they could have been taught English. It would also have helped if the parents had been taught English in evening classes so that they could speak English to their children and so help them to get on at school.

Some politicians used the immigrant question to win popularity. Peter Griffiths, a candidate in the 1964 election, said that he did not want Smethwick, his constituency, to become "a dumping ground for criminals, the chronic sick, and those who had no intention of working," suggesting that coloured immigrants were like this. In fact several surveys showed that in proportion to their numbers the coloured immigrants were more law-abiding than the native-born British.

It became clear in 1961 and 1962 that Britain could not allow a continuing influx of coloured immigrants. There were not enough houses for them, and it was feared that there would soon be fewer jobs for them as automation developed and white workers were dismissed. In 1962 the Conservative government passed the Commonwealth Immigration Act, which limited the number of immigrants allowed into Britain. Patrick Gordon Walker was the main speaker for the Labour Party, when it opposed this in the House of Commons.

Edward Short, Minister of Education, visiting a school in Wolverhampton, a town where there has been much trouble over racial integration

On the left dockers are seen marching on the House of Commons on 23 April 1968. They were demonstrating in support of Enoch Powell, who had just been sacked as Tory defence spokesman, and in protest against the government's Race Relations bill

Many coloured people find it difficult to get jobs. There is even discrimination between coloured people of different nationalities. This Ceylonese girl has found herself a reasonable job as a hairdresser

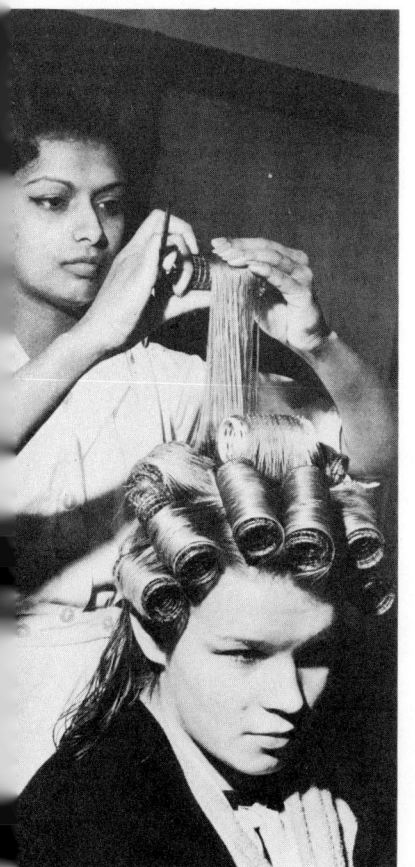

In 1965 the Labour government found that it could not keep its promise to be more generous than the Conservatives, and passed an Act restricting the number of Commonwealth Immigrants to 8,500 per year. Both the Conservative and Labour governments have insisted that once people have settled here, they and their children are to be treated as British citizens. There was a good deal of evidence that coloured people were barred from buying certain houses or getting certain jobs because of their colour. This, and other forms of discrimination, was made illegal by the Race Relations Act (1965).

In the near future there will be thousands of coloured boys and girls leaving British schools, colleges and universities. They will be the first generation of coloured Britishers. The way they are treated will determine whether or not Britain has a colour problem like that of the USA. Some people are not very hopeful. "Robert Blake, 18, has just spent a fortnight looking for a job. He qualified at a London grammar school for university entrance. The companies he approached wanted staff, but he is black, and almost none of them was interested. Two white friends tried for the same jobs. The employment agency that rejected Robert inside a minute gave them a 45-minute interview, called them 'excellent material' and started phoning employers. Robert's interview tended to be shorter than theirs. Everyone was polite, but told him he was late in applying, that there were a lot of other applicants.

A recent survey of an immigrant area in Birmingham showed a youngster is five times more likely to get a skilled job if he is white than if he is coloured. The chief youth employment officer in another Midlands city put it: "There is no problem for coloured youngsters at all—provided they realise what their abilities are. The question that no-one is trying to answer is whether this means that if you're black, you're second class."

Chapter nineteen
Education

Pre-war inequality

In 1931, Professor R. H. Tawney wrote: "The classless society is one in which people would enjoy similar standards of education..." [Chapter 12]. When he wrote, there were two different kinds of education; one was free, the other was not. Free education was provided in council "elementary" schools for children between the ages of five and fourteen. Parents who could afford it paid for their children to go to one or other of the many different sorts of fee-paying schools. These schools varied in size and cost—from the small, private school with perhaps as few as fifteen pupils, to Eton, with over 1,000 pupils—and included the grammar schools. About 15 per cent of the children in the grammar schools were "scholarship" children, their fees paid by a local council. The rest of the grammar school children paid fees. John Gunther wrote: "Before the war if a boy's father was a coal miner the chances were that the youngster would follow him; only exceptionally gifted, aggressive or lucky people emerged from their environment..."

Broadcasting to the nation in 1943 Mr Churchill said: "We must make sure that the path to the highest functions throughout our society and empire is really open to the children of every family." Before the War "the path" had been "open to the children..." who had gone to the fee-paying schools and to the fee-paying colleges and universities.

The 1944 Education Act

In 1943 the Beveridge Report named the "Giant Evils." In 1944, Mr R. A. Butler piloted an Education Act through Parliament which promised to cure one of them—Ignorance.

Many proposals in this Act have still not been carried out. In particular, Britain still does not have the nursery schools that this Act promised. But most of the Act has been put into effect.

This view of a school in 1869 contrasts sharply with the pictures on the opposite page

Girls in a modern comprehensive school

Britain has an educational system of free primary schools for children up to the age of eleven, followed by free secondary schools for all older children. The 1944 Act introduced the system of grants which makes it possible for any boy or girl of sufficient ability to go from school to college or university.

Educational reform and the economy

Many industrialists and politicians agreed with Churchill when he said in 1943 that: "The future of the world will be in the hands of the highly educated races, who alone can handle the scientific apparatus necessary for pre-eminence in peace or survival in war. You cannot conduct a modern community except with an adequate supply of persons upon whose education much time and money has been spent." Since 1943 the "scientific apparatus" has become even more complicated and larger than it was then; a modern country needs an even greater supply of educated workpeople. The growth in the number of children taking GCE (established in 1951) and CSE (established in 1965), is an indication of the willingness of boys and girls to become qualified, and of the demand by employers for more well-educated people.

Sixth form boys break for tea

Students in the hall of the Mechanical Engineering Department of the Imperial College of Science and Technology, London

Technology

Lord Bowden, the Head of the Manchester College of Technology, said: "For the first time in recorded history the survival of the country depends upon the universities." The earlier industrial revolutions had depended on the inventive genius of a few men such as the Stephensons who had developed the railway engine. Neither of them had even been to school; they, and many other early industrialists, learned by "doing" rather than out of books.

By the end of the nineteenth century new industries were developing—particularly chemicals and electrical engineering, in which the Germans and the Americans, who realised that technical education was the key to expansion, took the lead. In 1916 Lord Haldane, speaking in the House of Lords, said: "We suffer from want of experts. . . . It is no use saying to the manufacturers, 'Employ more chemists.' There are no chemists. Our training machine is not adquate to produce the supply we require."

Britain's economic decline was evident to many people before 1914. Sir Joseph Swan, a founder of the electric lamp industry, said in London in 1903: "We see one of the evil consequences of our educational deficiencies in the much less rapid progress that we have made in those branches of industry which are the outcome of the scientific discoveries of recent times. These depend on original research, and on the intelligent appreciation, by the capitalist and commercial class, of the resources of science and the advantages of scientific training and scientific work as forces in promoting industrial progress."

In 1957 Britain had fewer universities in proportion to its population than any other European country except Turkey. Since then the government has started new universities—at Brighton, Canterbury, Norwich, Colchester, York, Lancaster and Warwick.

British universities had produced great scientists, such as Lord Rutherford and Sir Alexander Fleming, but in the past had produced too few people qualified to apply the discoveries of pure scientists like them. The Germans and the Americans had founded special polytechnics in the late nineteenth century to train such applied scientists. Britain was slow to follow their example, and so fell behind in the development of new industries.

British universities tended to concentrate their attention on producing pure scientists rather than technologists. Imperial College, London, had struggled since 1907 to encourage a wider interest in technology. In 1953 the Conservative government decided to double the size of this college, but in 1966, the college authorities were still complaining about the low status of engineering in Britain. In France the Polytechnique (which trained engineers) was the pinnacle of ambition for clever schoolboys. In America there was a comparable glamour attached to

An old-fashioned school in London

the Massachussetts Institute of Technology. But in Britain, engineering is still looked on as a career for less able boys. The best boys, if they go into science at all, go into pure science.

In the mid-1950s, Lord Woolton persuaded the government to take an interest in the development of Colleges of Advanced Technology (CATs). In his *Memoirs* he wrote: "Sir James Chadwick told me that we would never get Britain into her right position until we had trained engineers capable of applying the results of laboratory research to industrial production. Chadwick convinced me that the country needed a clear lead from the government in the scientific training of technological engineers.

I determined to use the power my office gave me . . . and . . . the Cabinet finally agreed that we would develop in London, in Manchester and in Glasgow, three new Colleges of Science and Technology."

Comprehensives

The country needs an increasing number of technicians, technologists and graduates. This need will be fulfilled only if there are more boys and girls qualified for higher education. In 1944 fee-paying was abolished in the grammar schools; clever working-class children, it was hoped, would go to grammar

A modern, well-equipped school in Colchester

schools and help to meet the country's demand for qualified people. But Mrs H. R. Chetwynd, a teacher in South-East London in 1945, wrote saying: "It just didn't work out. In a street there are a dozen children approaching eleven-plus who have been friends since they were five. Probably all the parents are hoping their child will get to grammar school. Primary school head teachers are asked to provide a great deal of English, arithmetic and even intelligence, for many people believe this can be taught. Parents compare marks, help with homework, arrange extra coaching. Then, after the exam., three or four lucky boys and girls go to the schools everyone wants, and the rest, who have failed, go to the other schools."

The eleven-plus examination came under increasing attack throughout the 1950s and 1960s. One study showed that over one-third of all Welsh children went on to grammar schools, while only 15 per cent of Surrey children did so. The reason for this difference was not that Welsh children are on average over twice as clever as Surrey children, but that there happen to be a large number of old grammar schools in Wales. In Wales and in Surrey (and everywhere else) the eleven-plus examination was used to fill the empty desks in the local grammar schools, however many there were.

Reports of the differences in the percentage of eleven-plus "passes" in Wales and Surrey suggested that there was a large number of clever children not going to grammar schools in Surrey. This was a waste of talent which the country could not afford. Even more disturbing was a survey carried out by J.W.B. Douglas, who studied the educational performance of every child born in a week of March 1946. His survey showed that children of middle-class parents (in general people who had themselves had a grammar school education or better) had an advantage over working-class children of equal intelligence.

Other surveys showed that the eleven-plus examination was not in fact picking "the right children; out of every twenty children picked by the grammar school, six or seven turn out to be unsuited . . . and keep out six or seven of the remaining eighty who should have been admitted." One proof of the ability of "the failures" was the growth in the number of children in secondary modern (non-grammar) schools who were passing the GCE examination.

The Youth Employment Officer is well known to school leavers. He talks to individuals and groups, and tries to find suitable jobs for them

The range of school activities has grown enormously since the War. Above, domestic science in a comprehensive school; below, an open plan craft block

These were the main arguments used by people who opposed the eleven-plus examination system. They proposed a variety of secondary school systems which would do away with selection at the age of eleven. Some areas followed the Leicester Plan of junior and senior high schools; others started sixth form colleges. The most controversial were the large, all-in comprehensive schools, such as those established by the London County Council. The first, Kidbrooke, was opened in 1954 with 1,700 girls. The *News Chronicle* called it "A Palace of Learning," the *Evening Standard* "A Sausage Machine."

In 1968, out of a hundred and forty-eight Local Education Authorities (LEAs), sixty-five had definite plans for abolishing the eleven-plus system, fifty-five had set up committees to examine ways in which this could be done. The Labour government sent out a circular telling all LEAs to submit plans for the reorganisation of their secondary school systems, which would show how they intended to abolish eleven-plus selection. The former Conservative spokesman on Education, Sir Edward Boyle, made it clear that while he would not compel an Authority to change its secondary school system, he thought that the old selection system should be abandoned.

By the end of the 1960s Britain had moved a long way towards that classless society of which Tawney wrote. Early in 1970 the Donnisson Report said that fee-paying direct grant schools should become either completely independent, fee-paying schools or completely State-aided schools, forming part of whatever comprehensive system operates in each school's neighbourhood. Many of these schools will join the ranks of the public and independent schools, entry into which depends on wealth rather than ability. However, entrance to grammar schools, colleges and universities depends on intelligence rather than on money. One of the first actions of the newly-elected government (June 1970) was to announce its support for local authorities who wished to retain their grammar schools and selection examinations.

Chapter twenty
Communications

Radio

In *Our Times* (1953) Vivian Ogilvie wrote: "The first time I heard the wireless was in Wedmore, Somerset, in the late 1920s. A couple of men came to give a demonstration to us yokels. The sound was poor. Every now and then something would go wrong: not a very impressive performance. As we left the hall, the older people wagged their heads and declared that nothing would come of it.

Within months aerials were appearing on one house after another and the first question when you met anyone was: 'Have you got a wireless?' All over the country, as though from nowhere, hordes of young mechanics were available to install a set, to build a set and to attend to repairs."

By 1939 there were nearly nine million radio licence holders, although there were many homes without a radio. In 1947 the number of licence holders reached eleven million—a proof of the increasing affluence of our society—and a peak was reached in 1950, when nearly twelve million licences were bought.

The influence of radio has been enormous. On the one hand it has had an educational value, as Ogilvie noted: "In talks and school broadcasts the BBC went further than any other radio organisation in the world. It developed radio drama. Outside broadcasts have expanded the magazine side of broadcasting. Documentaries, features and discussion have provided new ways of putting over information. Games and entertainments have been devised."

Then it has provided millions of hours of light entertainment. Millions of listeners have followed the fortunes of the Dales, the Archers, Paul Temple, and have laughed with Tony Hancock, Frankie Howerd and Jimmy Edwards.

The transistor was invented as part of the development of the computer industry to replace the bulkier valve, and it was soon used by radio manufacturers to provide cheap, portable radios, bought in large numbers by younger people anxious to listen to the new Pop Record programmes. This demand for record programmes led to the setting up of "pirate" commercial radio stations, and in 1970 to the reform in the BBC structure. Local BBC radio stations were introduced to provide items of local interest as well as a good deal of pop music; BBC One was begun as an alternative to the pirate commercial stations, to cater for the pop fan.

Television

In 1950 there were only 343,000 television sets licensed in

Rapid progress in space research has resulted in close links between continents by communications satellites. Here is the ELDO *Europa* 1 satellite launcher

105

Britain. Technological developments in the early 1950s helped manufacturers to provide cheaper sets, and because of increasing affluence many British workers could afford either to buy or to rent a set. By 1965 over thirteen million sets were licensed, so that the BBC and commercial television companies estimate that they can now reach about 96 per cent of the British population.

Up to 1954 only the BBC was allowed to produce television programmes. The Conservative government decided to end this monopoly and set up the Independent Television Authority,

Three generations of computer technology: vacuum tube array, transistor card and SLT modules

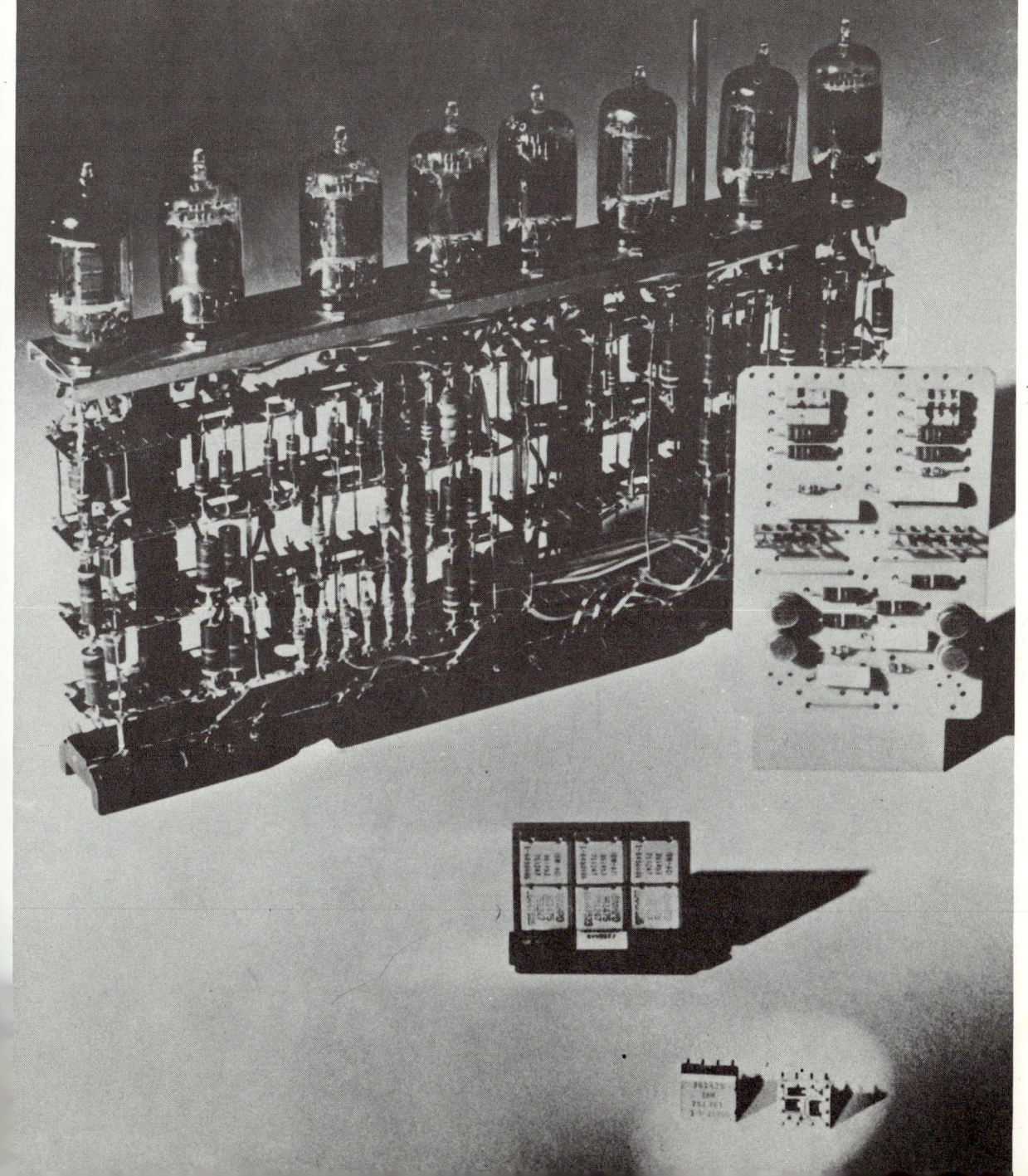

Philip Harben tossing a pancake on television

The BBC television centre, Wood Lane, London

to supervise new television companies (Granada, Associated Television, Westward Television etc.) The BBC gets the money it needs from licence fees; these new companies get their money from advertising. Some people opposed this step. Lord Samuels, speaking in the House of Lords said: "Our modern twentieth-century civilisation is already far too much commercialised by the buying and selling of things that we use and consume. Advertisements have been intrusive everywhere for the last fifty years . . . Now we have this new influence entering every home and affecting the environment of every family. Why should we, for the sake of picking up a million or two, degrade our broadcasting system with a continuous stream of commercial advertising? . . . Once you let in this principle, it is almost impossible to stop it because the financial advantage is so enormous; sponsored broadcasts must, sooner or later, dominate a large part of the programmes, and leave to the BBC the less remunerative ones."

Others felt that commercialisation would lead to a lowering of standards on television. They pointed to the example of the USA where the programmes are of a poorer quality than those shown on BBC. However, there is no evidence that this has happened, although many people feel that the most popular programmes, such as those illustrated here, lack any serious content.

Commercial television flourished because manufacturers spent increasing amounts on advertising all their products. This advertising is a sign of increasing affluence—manufacturers advertise because they expect to sell their goods; they spent more on advertising as time went on because they expected to sell more to the affluent British.

One of BBC television's most popular panel games, *What's my Line?* From left to right: Isobel Barnett, Ted Moult, Sara Leighton, Gilbert Harding

Newspapers

The newspapers were another sign of this affluence. In the 1940s newspaper owners were allowed to import only a limited quantity of pulp and paper. Newspapers were smaller than they had been in 1939. Four and six page editions of the daily papers had little space for advertisements, and in the days of shortage and rationing, advertisers were not looking for a great deal of space. But in the more affluent Britain of the late 1950s and 1960s, newspapers became larger as the advertisers bought more and more space. By 1968 newspaper owners depended on their advertisers for about half their revenue. In order to attract even more advertisements, women's magazines and daily papers grew larger, although they never reached the hundred and twenty pages of the American paper. Some of the newspapers (the *Sunday Times, Daily Telegraph* and *Observer*) published special colour supplements, consisting mainly of advertisements, to distribute free to their readers.

Air travel

Before 1939 air travel was in its infancy. Several companies operated flights inside Britain and between Britain and Europe. But there were no regular flights across the Atlantic; such flights were left to popular hero figures like Amelia Ehrhart and the Mollisons. The war saw a great improvement in the design of aircraft and engines, in communication between ground and air, in the training of crews. Once the war was over, airline companies recruited former bomber and fighter pilots, used old RAF and USAF planes, and began to provide air services over the Atlantic and to the Far East.

In 1946, Geoffrey de Havilland, a British test pilot, broke through the sound barrier when he put his plane into a dive and reached supersonic speed. His plane broke up and he died, but he had shown the way to other men. Improved engines and airframes were designed and on 14 October 1947 Captain Charles Yaeger of the United States Air Force achieved the first level supersonic flight when he flew a Bell XS-1 rocket plane over the Edwards Air Force Base, California, at an altitude of 42,000 feet.

The Anglo-French *Concorde*. It is a supersonic aeroplane. Its nose gives the wings greater lift at low speeds, and when lowered gives the pilot better visibility for landing

Geoffrey de Havilland was only one of many who were trying to give Britain a lead in the air age. Frank Whittle had invented the jet engine in 1937, and in May 1941 his *Gloster E.*28, fitted with a turbo-jet engine, achieved a speed of 370 mph. By the end of the war, jets had fought on both sides—the *Gloster* designed by Whittle and the German *M.E.*262.

British aircraft manufacturers went ahead, after 1945, with attempts to produce a commercial plane using jet engines. De Havilland produced the *Comet* which was bought by BOAC and used on scheduled services from 2 May 1953. The *Comet* had a cruising speed of 500 mph and could reach Tokyo within thirty-six hours of leaving London.

The headline writers were unanimous in their opinion that the *Comet* was Britain's greatest technological breakthrough of the century. Foreign airlines rushed to book orders for the new *Comet*, which had gone through a series of severe tests before being put into commercial use, and seemed to have none of the teething troubles which new planes often have.

Then, on 10 January 1954, a *Comet* on the Rome-London route exploded over the Isle of Elba. Twenty-three passengers were lost. A few weeks later, another came down off the coast of Italy and twenty-one people died. All other *Comets* were grounded and their certificates of airworthiness were withdrawn. It was February 1955 before it was decided that the probable cause of the disaster was a failure of the pressure cabins due to metal fatigue. A weak point in the airliner's thin metal skin was unable to stand up to the strains of pressurisation at great heights. De Havilland made the necessary changes and a larger, more powerful *Comet* was produced, but by that time the five-year lead that Britain had boasted of had almost entirely disappeared, and American aircraft manufacturers such as Douglas, and Boeing, were producing cheaper aircraft of similar design and greater capability.

The affluent British began to travel by air on business and for pleasure; foreign tourists came by air in increasing numbers, so that in the late 1960s London's two airports—Gatwick and

BOAC's VC10

Heathrow—were unable to deal with the volume of traffic. This led to the demand for a third airport. The need for this has become increasingly evident now that the new Jumbo-jets are crossing the Atlantic, bringing four or five hundred passengers at a time.

The Hovercraft

Although Britain played little part in the development of rockets and space flight, it did produce a new means of transport. In July 1959, the Saunders Roe Company's Hovercraft arrived at Dover beach after skimming across the English Channel from Calais in two hours and three minutes, exactly fifty years after Blériot first flew from France to England.

Christopher Cockerell, the inventor of the Hovercraft, turned to boatbuilding after being a successful electronics engineer with Marconi. By 1955 he had hawked his theories round the aircraft and shipping industries but received no solid backing. He realised that the only convincing way to get anyone really interested would be to build a working model. This he took to the Admiralty and the Ministry of Supply where it was promptly classified as "secret." No further development seemed possible.

In 1957 he discovered that a Swiss engineer was working on a similar machine. He determined to gain clearance for the Hovercraft and received permission to approach the National Development Corporation. Meanwhile Saunders Roe, who had been given a small contract by the Ministry of Supply to develop Cockerell's findings, now decided that the Hovercraft could be released for commercial rather than military development.

In 1959 the Hovercraft Development Company Limited was formed, financed—at last—by the Treasury.

The Hovercraft, which now makes regular journeys between Britain and the Continent

Rail travel

When the railways were nationalised (January 1948) the government realised that vast sums of public money would have to be spent on re-equipping them. Locomotives and rolling stock had deteriorated through lack of maintenance during the War, and many bridges, stations and sections of track were in a shocking state of repair.

A new series of British Railways Standard steam locomotives was introduced (1951). But by the time the last of them was built– a goods engine named *Evening Star* (March 1960)—diesel and electric locomotives were taking over from steam. In 1955 there were 19,000 steam-engines in operation, eight years later numbers had dropped below 7,000. However, diesel and electric trains were cleaner, more efficient and required much less servicing between runs. Electric trains in particular can start and stop very quickly. This made them a great asset on the crowded Southern Region suburban services, which were largely electrified by 1939. The great cost of electrification prevented other regions from following the example of the Southern much earlier than the 1950s and 1960s.

Road transport continued to capture traffic from the railways, especially freight. To enable railways to compete on more equal terms, a massive Modernisation Plan was introduced in 1954. The building of diesel and electric engines was speeded up, stations and marshalling yards were remodelled, and local passenger services that lost money were reduced or discontinued. Britain's railway network, which reached a peak of 20,405 route miles in 1930, had come down to 17,000 miles by 1963. In that year further drastic cuts were proposed by a special Committee of Inquiry under Dr Reginald Beeching. To reduce British Rail's enormous losses (£87 million in 1962), Beeching advised that a further 5,000 miles of unprofitable lines should be closed. At the same time, traffic would be built up on well-loaded routes, mainly long-distance freight and passenger runs, and the daily suburban services of large towns. But the government stopped the full swing of the "Beeching Axe" in the interests of certain country areas where railways were the main contact with the outside world.

One of the diesel trains designed to make rail travel faster and more economic

The M6 motorway, one of the many motorways built to cope with increasing traffic in a country where more and more people own cars

Motor travel

Between 1951 and 1960 the number of road vehicles doubled, and during the prosperous 1960s the figure doubled again; by 1970 nearly twelve million private cars crowded the roads. This has created a problem for British towns and cities—where are all these cars to be parked? Coin meters were introduced to discourage motorists from parking for long periods, more off-street parking space was built by local authorities. Some people believe that, in the future, the motor-car will have to be banned from the town and city centres and that free, efficient public transport will have to be provided to cater for those who wish to travel in these areas. Other people believe that the centres of British towns and cities will have to be redesigned, at very great cost, to allow the private motorist freedom to travel and park.

One of the signs of the affluent society was the building of the new Motorways. The first—the M1—is a six-lane dual carriageway running for over sixty miles between London and Birmingham. This was opened in 1959. Since then over four hundred miles of motorways have been built and are in use. However, Britain is still a long way behind other industrialised countries where roads of this kind had been built in the 1930s.

Chapter twenty-one
Entertainment

Cinemas

In 1946 there were over 4,750 cinemas in Britain and just over thirty million people went to the cinema each week. By 1967 there were under 2,000 cinemas and only five million people went. The film producers have tried to recapture some of the lost audience. In the early 1950s cinemas presented the miracles of Cinemascope, Vista Vision, 3D (in which audiences watched films through rose-coloured spectacles), Todd-AO or Cinerama. They made very expensive films such as *Around the World in Eighty Days,* in which Michael Todd launched Todd-AO with an all-star cast, or Cecil de Mille's wide screen *Ten Commandments.*

Some American producers managed to attract huge audiences to such films, and to musicals such as *My Fair Lady, The Sound of Music,* and *South Pacific.* But in general people preferred to stay at home and watch their television sets. British film studios at Denham, Shepherds Bush, Ealing, Teddington and Wembley were either closed or were converted to making films for television.

Film makers had used female stars to attract large audiences in the past; Mary Pickford was a star of the silent screen in the early 1900s; Jean Harlow and Mae West were two of the stars of the 1930s; Marilyn Monroe and Jane Russell used their vital statistics to become film stars. But in 1960 an Italian producer Fellini, made *La Dolce Vita* (*The Sweet Life*), which told the story

The King and I **was the film version of a spectacular American musical,** *Anna and the King of Siam*

Three-dimensional films made going to the cinema sometimes over-realistic. But the fashion for them did not last long

of the decadence of modern Rome. It caused great scandal in Italy, particularly at the Vatican. It also attracted large audiences all over the world. Other film producers realised that such films could make a good deal of money and so British screens were filled with Swedish, French, Danish and German pornographic films, while British producers tried to make similar films, e.g. *Up the Junction, Poor Cow,* etc.

Some people tried to justify the making of such films, arguing that they were reflections of modern society; one Churchman described *La Dolce Vita* as a modern parable; another thought that it portrayed the boredom of sinning. The cinema screen, like the theatre and television, became a medium for writers and producers who wanted to tell people more about society. In *If*, the producer tried to support the argument for the abolition of old-fashioned discipline in the public schools; in *Oh, What a Lovely War*, the cinema-goer had a chance to share with playgoers at the Royal Court Theatre the anti-war ideas of Miss Joan Littlewood.

However, the cinema failed to hold its large audiences. Many cinemas were converted into Bingo Halls after the Betting and Gaming Act, 1960, had made Bingo Clubs legal. In 1968 there were over seven million Bingo players in the country, many of whom went to play two or three times a week.

Inside a bingo club

Theatre

Immediately after 1945 British theatres were invaded by a Succession of spectacular American musicals: *Annie Get Your Gun, Oklahoma, South Pacific,* were later followed by *Anna and the King of Siam* (later filmed as *The King and I*), *West Side Story* and *My Fair Lady*. British writers have imitated their American cousins and have provided shows such as *Oliver* for the musical theatre.

In 1956 John Osborne's play *Look Back in Anger* was produced at the Royal Court Theatre, London. *The Times*' critic said: "... The piece consists largely of angry tirades, The hero regards himself, and is clearly regarded by the author, as the specimen for the younger post-war generation which looks round at the world and finds nothing right with it." Osborne's was the first of a series of plays by British playwrights who became known as the Angry Young Men. Wesker, Pinter and Beckett wrote plays which attacked the existing social system, challenged long-held beliefs on behaviour and morality. *Waiting for Godot* was written by Beckett, an Irish playwright living in Paris. During the whole of the play the stage is taken up by only two tramps, whose concern seems to be to show the audience the stupidity of living at all. Who the Godot is for whom they are waiting was never made clear, and critics were as mystified as the audience.

This attack on the existing social system was welcomed by young people and by liberal critics and writers. They saw this freedom of criticism as part of the campaign for freedom. The high spot of their campaign was reached in 1969. The highlight of the year was the staging of *Oh, Calcutta!* in New York.

Much of the money that teenagers have in the affluent 70s is spent on records

Although a critic for *The Times* felt that *Oh, Calcutta!* was "the kind of show to give pornography a dirty name" and on 22 June the *Observer* commented: "I never thought I would live to see anything like this. It is unbelievable, quite unbelievable," *Oh, Calcutta!* shows every sign of continuing. ". . . This week's performances have been to packed houses with long lines of people hopefully waiting for returned tickets—although the theatre is ancient and uncomfortable and in an unfashionable part of town . . ."

With the help of grants from the government the Arts Council has helped local enthusiasts to found new local theatres at Nottingham, Coventry, Bristol, Leatherhead and Croydon. The Labour government included a new Minister for Arts: Miss Jennie Lee, who held this post from 1964 to 1970, succeeded in getting increasing sums of money from Labour Chancellors to support local efforts, which means that more people have a chance to see a play.

Books and records

A more educated and affluent people have shown increasing willingness to support the theatre. They have also borrowed millions of books from their local libraries, as well as buying vast numbers of paper-back books on all sorts of subjects. Allen Lane was the founder of the paper-back movement when he started Penguin Books in 1936. Since 1945, Penguins have been joined by Pelicans and Puffins, Mayflower and Pan, Fontana and Four Square, and every subject from algebra to Zen Buddhism has its paper-back literature.

Through the wireless and television an ever-increasing number of people have learned to enjoy serious music, as the sale of Long-Playing records shows. The LP was invented in 1950 to allow a whole symphony to be recorded on two sides. Although there is still a demand for such records, and for long-playing discs made by old-fashioned dance bands, and "squarer" singers such as Val Doonican, the bulk of LPs are made by the pop artists, and the sale of millions of these records indicates both the affluence of the British buyers and the source of much of their entertainment.

Sport

Sport has remained a major form of entertainment. When the Olympic Games were held in London in 1948 British athletes took no honours. Since then, British athletes have become more successful, and Gordon Pirie, Bruce Tulloh, Christopher Chataway have become household names. No British athlete was better known than Roger Bannister, who broke the four-minute mile, a goal about which milers had dreamed for years. Twenty-five-year old Bannister set up the new world record at Iffley Road, Oxford, on 6 May 1954. Two of his opponents—and pace-mates—were Chris Chataway, now Conservative MP for Chich-

Yachting is a sport which before the War was too expensive for most people. Affluence has brought it within the reach of far more people. The yacht here is a *Triton*

ester, and Chris Brasher. The race had been planned with scrupulous care; Brasher made the running for two and a half laps, then Chataway took over before Bannister made his final, historical effort with 230 yards to go. He finished the race in 3 mins. 59.4 secs. Australian athlete John Landy, who became Bannister's greatest rival, succeeded in breaking his record on 21 June the same year, finishing in a time of 3 mins. 57.9 secs.

In 1950 the English football team was beaten 1-0 in a World Cup match, by the United States, and in 1953 Hungary became the first foreign team to defeat England at home. However, Britain re-established herself as the world's leading soccer nation in 1966 by winning the World Cup, and English clubs have followed the example of Scotland's Celtic in winning major European competitions.

English cricket recovered from the effects of the War, although Brian Glanville wrote: "1950 was the year of the West Indian cricket tour, of calypso . . . Ramadhin and Valentine, of West Indians streaming in joyful triumph across the hallowed turf of Lord's after the Second Test had been won. . . . 'The bowling was super fine . . . Ramadhin and Valentine!' Both were spin bowlers. Sonny Ramadhin a tiny tricky fellow of just twenty, whose cunning leg-breaks were often unplayable that summer. Alf Valentine taller and graver, a few days older, who did almost as much damage at the other end. Then the batsmen: the graceful

Roger Bannister breaking the record for the mile. He was the first man to run a mile in under four minutes

Celebrations after the defeat of England by the West Indians in 1950

World Cup victory for England in 1966

Worrell, the calm Stollmeyer, the colossally powerful Everton Weeks, Clyde Walcott the wicket-keeper and run-maker. They won the rubber 3–1, investing a tired old game with new colour and excitement..."

Cricket became a major talking point in 1968, when the South African government refused to allow the MCC to take a coloured player, Basil d'Oliveira, to South Africa—where he had been born and from which he had emigrated to try to lead a fuller life in Britain. This policy of apartheid led many to support the demonstrations against the South African Rugby tourists in the winter of 1969/70 and the South African cricket tour of 1970. The young demonstrators believe that they have a right to show the South Africans that many British people are opposed to a policy which prevents a coloured South African having the same rights as a white man.

One of the main developments of post-War Britain has been the growth in the number of people taking part in activities such as yachting, golfing, swimming, motor rallying, which are non-team sports. Once these had been the privilege of the wealthier middle and upper classes. The more affluent worker now finds that he can afford these things along with increasing numbers of middle class, and in 1964 the government appointed a Ministry of Sport.

Chapter twenty-two
Holidaying Britons

In the middle of the British winter the newspapers are full of pictures put out by tourist agencies advertising holidays in sunny Spain, glamorous Greece and romantic Italy. These advertisements are paid for by agents who know that in the summer they will be collecting money from millions of Britishers seeking the sun on a foreign holiday. This is one aspect of the social revolution of post-War Britain.

Seaside holidays

In 1936 only one and a half million manual workers were getting a week's paid holiday: over ten million workers had no paid holiday at all. In 1938 the government passed the Holidays with Pay Act, which did not force but encouraged employers to give all their workpeople at least one week's holiday with pay. By June 1939 eleven million workers had been given this privilege; since then the length of the holiday has increased. In 1948 three million and in 1956 over twelve million workers were getting two weeks' paid holiday. Now trade unions are asking for three weeks' holiday with pay, and over two million people take one holiday in the summer and another in the winter.

At first the working classes followed the middle-class pattern of going to the seaside for their holidays. Billy Butlin opened his first holiday camp at Skegness in 1937 and by 1939 there were over one hundred such holiday camps in different parts of the country. Since 1945 British seaside resorts, such as Blackpool, have expanded to cater for the ever-increasing numbers of holiday-makers. Holiday camps have become more and more luxurious, in their attempts to attract more of the affluent workers, while whole areas of Britain have learned to cater for the new working-class holiday-maker. Cornwall had its first large-scale invasion by Lancashire workers in 1953; since then, Cornwall, Scotland, North Wales, the Lake District and other remote parts have gained from the influx of working-class holiday-makers.

As the worker became more affluent and more eager to see other areas of his own country, manufacturers came to his aid by producing better and better camping equipment. Once upon a time camping had been something done by Boy Scouts or hardy people willing to face cold and damp. Today, with quilted beds and modern cooking equipment, separate rooms in tents and special furniture, camping is almost an extension of suburban living.

Other manufacturers have provided caravans and motorised caravans. These can be seen in ever-increasing numbers on the

The famous tower at Blackpool, one of Britain's most famous holiday towns

Butlin's holiday camp at Clacton. An increasing number of people spent their holidays in such camps in the 1940s and 1950s. In the 1960s, more people went abroad for their holidays, and camps such as this became less popular

Camping at Postbridge on Dartmoor. In the affluent society more and more people use sites such as this for week-ends and holidays

British roads in the summer. These, and the tents, allow people to enjoy the privilege of week-ending away from home, as well as being an aid to the enjoyment of a longer holiday. Instead of going to "the seaside" for a week or two, more and more people now tour the West Country, the Lake District or Scotland, stopping for a night on a camping site where water, washing and shopping facilities are available.

Every tourist who goes abroad spends foreign currency and so adds to the import side of the British balance of payments. As more people go abroad so the amount spent increases, although it has to be remembered that this is a two-way traffic, and that the foreign tourists who visit Britain in ever-increasing numbers add to the export side of the balance of payments when they spend their currency here.

In the long term the habit of taking a foreign holiday has its effects on the British way of life. French wines, German lagers, Italian pasta and Danish bread are only four of the many continental tastes that British tourists pick up. They ask for these things in their local shops, and as the demand grows the shops learn to provide the goods. This adds to the British imports bill since the wine and spaghetti have to be imported; it also adds to the quality of British life as more people enjoy a wider number of different kinds of food and drink.

As people become better-off they will try to spend more money on leisure and on holidays. Over two million people now take a second holiday each year—one in the summer and a second in the spring or winter. As time goes on this habit will spread, as will the habit of owning a country or seaside cottage. For the moment these are things which only the wealthier can afford. In time those who are at present less well off will have become wealthier and will wish to imitate their social superiors. These will then turn in ever-increasing numbers to join those who have bought their own holiday property in Malta or Spain or Portugal or some other sunny country.

Foreign holidays

The upper classes had long ago taken holidays abroad but in September 1953 *The Times* reported: "The artisan, the typist, the clerk and the shop assistant are discovering France, Switzerland, Spain and Italy."

In 1955 two million people went for a holiday abroad; in 1962 there were over four and a half million, when foreign travel accounted for one-third of the money spent on holidays.

There has been an increase in the number of tourist agencies to cater for the growing number of people wanting to go abroad for a holiday. At first they provided holidays in traditional centres, such as Spain, Southern France, Italy and Greece; in the mid-1950s they opened the beaches of Yugoslavia to British tourists for the first time and began to provide holidays in Africa, America and the Pacific Islands.

In 1966 the Labour government limited the amount of money which could be taken abroad to £50 per person. It was hoped that this would restrict the numbers going abroad, and so help our balance of payments. In fact, the evidence is that agencies suceeded in devising foreign holidays which the British holiday-maker could afford and they advertised these new, cheap foreign holidays and so attracted for the first time many people who had previously thought only of a holiday in Britain because they imagined that foreign holidays were too expensive. For the first time they realised that a holiday on the Costa Brava or in Majorca was as cheap as a holiday at Butlin's, and that the sun was more or less guaranteed.

Since the War, foreign restaurants have increased in popularity. Here is the Swiss Centre, in London, where the food, the decor, and the staff are Swiss

Chapter twenty-three
Fashion

Until the mid 1950s, fashion was created by a few important designers, like Dior and Balenciaga, in Paris, who made expensive clothes for very rich women; they sold copies of their dresses to firms such as Marks and Spencer's, who then mass-produced an imitation of the latest Paris fashion. Both the designers and the mass-producers tried to create clothes that would suit the customers with most money—the middle-aged women, who had finished the expensive business of bringing up children and who now had money to spare for new clothes.

Young people wore a cut-down version of the clothes worn by middle-aged people. No designer thought that young people deserved any special attention because few of them had much money.

Until 1952 clothes were rationed. When Princess Elizabeth and Lieutenant Philip Mountbatten were engaged in 1947 the *New York Times* wrote: "Depressing news continues to come from

Her Royal Highness Princess Elizabeth and the Duke of Edinburgh in July 1947. The style of her dress is having a come-back at the beginning of the 1970s

Summer fashion in 1948. Skirts were long and very, very full

austerity-ridden England. The latest—that Princess Elizabeth must forego her trousseau (her engagement to Lieutenant Philip Mountbatten had been announced the previous month)—will stir pity in the heart of every bride-to-be in America.

The Board of Trade had promised her all the coupons she needs. But her parents, after due consideration of the proprieties, have decreed that any special privilege for royalty would be out of place in the present Spartan conditions of English life . . ."

New Look, 1947

In 1947 Christian Dior, the famous Paris designer, produced dresses, skirts and coats that had long, swirling skirts, flounces, wasp waists and bustles. He said that in producing such feminine-looking clothes he was trying to get away from the drab, military-like clothes that women had worn for so long. The British government considered for a time legislating against this new length and fullness, which would use up more material than the older clothes; Sir Stafford Cripps, the Chancellor, appealed to women not to buy these luxuries; Miss Mabel Ridleagh, MP for North Ilford, speaking of the wasp-waist, said: ". . . it was too reminiscent of the 'caged bird attitude'. I hope our fashion dictators will realise the new *outlook* of women and give the death blow to any attempt at curtailing women's freedom."

However, events proved that Christian Dior was right and Miss Ridleagh wrong. In 1948 the British street scene was transformed: women in Carlisle and Cardiff, in Liverpool and in Leeds discarded their old clothes in favour of the new, curvier clothes. Firms which mass-produced women's clothes rushed to copy Dior's idea, much to the distress of moralists who declared that the fashion would have "an undesirable influence on the impressionable male," but to the delight of manufacturers of foundation garments—still, in 1947, called "luxury garments" by the Board of Trade, since only a small minority of women bought them.

Teddy Boys, 1948

Some wealthier young men of London's West End decided that men's fashion needed a change after the austerity of wartime. They began to wear narrowed trousers, velvet-collared jackets, brocaded waistcoats and pointed shoes. Like the New Look, this fashion spread from the London West End to the less wealthy parts of Britain, and for the next ten years the Teddy Boy was a feature of British society.

Young affluence, 1958

John Osborne's play *Look Back in Anger* was first produced in 1956, at the Royal Court Theatre. It set a pattern for other British playwrights in its demand for a revolt against tradition and authority. As if in response to this demand, there was an upsurge of British-produced fashion intended to be worn by the

The RAF Demobilisation Centre in Lancashire, where men were fitted out with civilian clothes

very young. In 1958 Mary Quant was one of the first to design clothes, shoes, make-up, hair styles for the under-20s, for whom London's Carnaby Street became a mecca.

New words (like "fab" and "gear") were used in new shops (like *Lord John's*) where "dolly" assistants waited to serve the affluent young. The clothes were simple and, above all, they were relatively cheap. In the 1940s, Dior and others had catered for the very rich, and the less well-to-do had imitated these fashions. In the late 1950s designers catered for the "classless" society of young people. The Dior revolutionary New Look had begun at the top of the income/age scale and then spread downwards: the Quant/Carnaby Street Revolution began with the young and spread upwards to older women, many of whom complained that they found it impossible to find a shop to provide them with the clothes they needed—everyone seemed to be catering for the young.

The mini-skirt

In 1966 the first of Britain's post-War babies were twenty-one years old. Their memories were of a continually improving life as rationing and shortages came to an end, and wages continually rose. In 1966 London designers produced the first mini-skirt; this New Look swept the country, and then was adopted by young people in Europe and America. The young fashion spread as older women followed the example of the young. In 1968 the Chancellor had to change the purchase tax regulations because older women were buying tax-free skirts meant for 14-year olds instead of the longer, purchase-taxed skirts meant for older women.

Swinging London

In 1968 tourist agencies in the United States advertised holidays in "Swinging London," declaring that London was now the centre of the youthful world. There were four and a half million people under the age of thirty living in Greater London. British dress designers, pop groups, playwrights, actors, were making a great impact on the world. James Laver has made a special study of women's clothes through the centuries. He believes that the mini-skirt and other modern fashions are a reflection of the freedom which modern women enjoy compared with their predecessors. They also reflect the greater affluence of the young of all classes.

Mary Quant, who turned from buying clothes to designing them, and has had a huge influence on young fashion

Boutiques such as this, exclusively for teenagers, are a very recent development. They grew up in the 1960s

Chapter twenty-four
Women and the family

Women and work

During the War millions of women were conscripted into the Armed Forces and millions of others took the place of men in factories and workshops. Married and single women went to work and brought an extra wage packet into the home, which gave their families a higher standard of living during the War than had been possible in the depressed 1930s.

Once the War was over some people thought that there would be a repetition of what had happened in the 1920s. Women had helped during the First World War (1914–18); but immediately the War ended, trade unions and government combined to get the women out of the factories and workshops and back into their homes. But since 1945 there has been a continued demand for more workers to help in the rebuilding of the country, to staff the growing welfare services, to produce the goods needed for exports. As the country recovered from the War there was increased demand for workers to produce goods for the affluent British who also wanted more shops, more services—and so more workers.

Women in the operations room of RAF Fighter Command

Women working in a tank factory in 1941. In the week when this photograph was taken the factory was aiming at a record output. The results were to be sent to Russia – so a greetings message is being painted in Russian on this tank

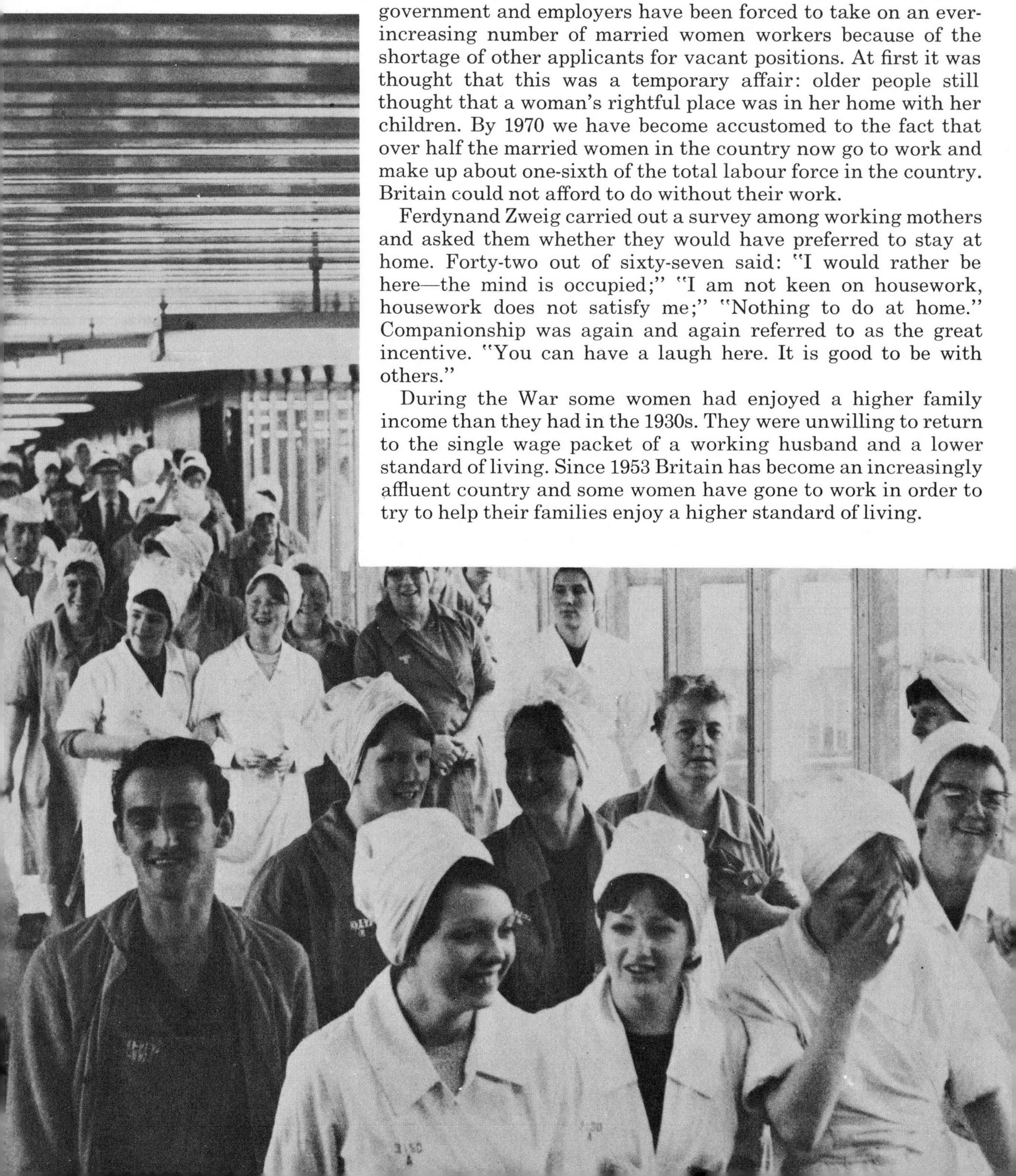

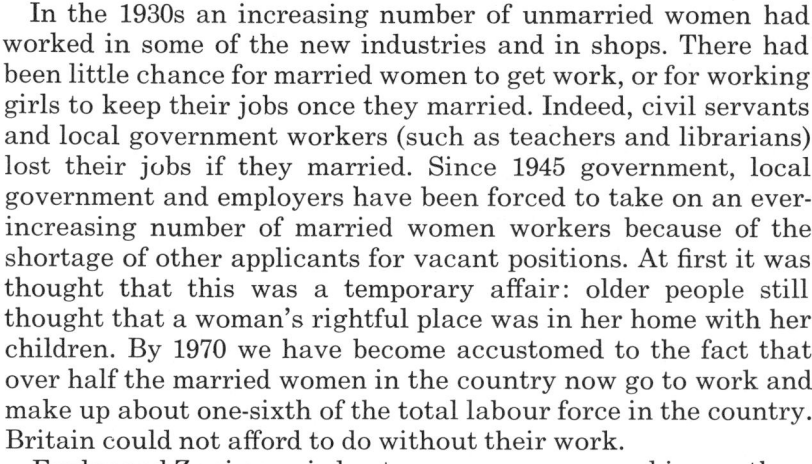

Women at work in the Heinz food factory in Lancashire – the biggest in Europe

In the 1930s an increasing number of unmarried women had worked in some of the new industries and in shops. There had been little chance for married women to get work, or for working girls to keep their jobs once they married. Indeed, civil servants and local government workers (such as teachers and librarians) lost their jobs if they married. Since 1945 government, local government and employers have been forced to take on an ever-increasing number of married women workers because of the shortage of other applicants for vacant positions. At first it was thought that this was a temporary affair: older people still thought that a woman's rightful place was in her home with her children. By 1970 we have become accustomed to the fact that over half the married women in the country now go to work and make up about one-sixth of the total labour force in the country. Britain could not afford to do without their work.

Ferdynand Zweig carried out a survey among working mothers and asked them whether they would have preferred to stay at home. Forty-two out of sixty-seven said: "I would rather be here—the mind is occupied;" "I am not keen on housework, housework does not satisfy me;" "Nothing to do at home." Companionship was again and again referred to as the great incentive. "You can have a laugh here. It is good to be with others."

During the War some women had enjoyed a higher family income than they had in the 1930s. They were unwilling to return to the single wage packet of a working husband and a lower standard of living. Since 1953 Britain has become an increasingly affluent country and some women have gone to work in order to try to help their families enjoy a higher standard of living.

Barbara Castle. It is thought by many that she may one day become Britain's first woman Prime Minister. She is speaking here at the 1967 Labour Party Conference which approved her decision to introduce an Equal Pay bill

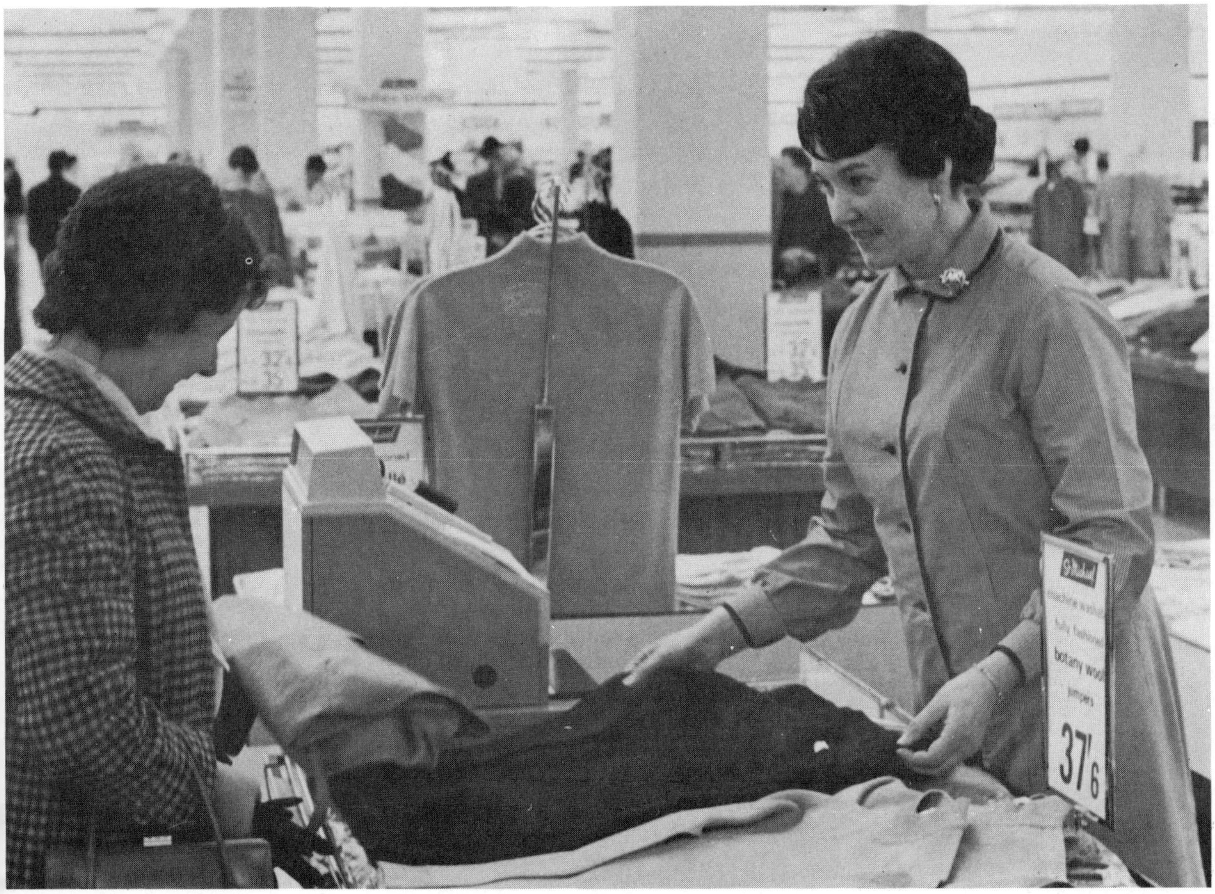

Women at work: an assistant at Marks and Spencer

Equal pay

In 1945 a working woman received on average 20 per cent less pay than the male worker doing the same job. Male trade unionists and male employers thought that men should get more than women, saying "after all, most men are married and have to support a family on their wage; women workers are either single and have no-one to keep but themselves, or they are married and their wage is just an extra for the family." Since 1945 women have campaigned for equal pay for equal work; their first success was in the teaching profession where there were more women than men. In 1955 the Teachers' Unions and the government agreed that men and women teachers were to get the same rates of pay. The Trade Union Congress had supported the women's campaign, although individual trade unions bargaining with individual employers were less enthusiastic. However, in 1969 Barbara Castle, Minister of Employment and Productivity, proposed in her Equal Pay Bill that from 1975 there should be no difference in the pay received by women and men workers doing the same job.

An unusual woman teacher, Anita Williams. Before starting to teach in England she travelled half way around the world. She finally came back to teach English in Eastbourne

Equal opportunity

This measure was opposed by those who thought that even if women appeared to be doing the same job as a man they could not be as efficient workers as men. Some argued that women are away sick more often than men; others that women have to leave their work to have babies, and so are of less use to an employer than a male worker. Others argue that women, particularly married women, could not do the overtime or the shift work that men do. Even in the professions there is still a feeling that women are not as good as men. Wendy Cooper reported in the *Daily Telegraph* in September 1966: "Miss Hess, Principal of the Studley Agricultural College for Women, was once an applicant for a headship of an important farming institute. She was told that she had the experience and qualifications needed, and could undoubtedly do the job, but... did she realise that 50 per cent of their students were men? Miss Hess asked: 'And what sex are the other 50 per cent?'"

This assumption that it is all right for men to teach women but not the other way round is one of the attitudes lingering on to impede women's progress.

In spite of this, however, there are still women who get to the top of their chosen profession. Barbara Castle is spoken of as "perhaps our first woman Prime Minister"—in which case British women will become equal to women in India and Israel which have already had women Prime Ministers. In 1965 Judge Elizabeth Lane became the first woman to be appointed to the High Court, but Britain still does not have women commercial pilots or ships' captains as Russia has.

Women at home and at work

Married women find it easier to go to work in the 1970s than they would have done even forty years ago. One of the reasons for this is that running a home is much easier with washing machines and spin dryers, clothes made out of synthetic fibres, and homes with polystyrene tiles and formica tables. Another important factor is the size of the family. Ferdynand Zweig interviewed 548 married men at five separate Works and found that most of them had only one or two children:

NUMBER OF FAMILIES WITH NUMBERS OF CHILDREN

	0	1–2	3	4 or more	Total
Sheffield	24	93	22	11	150
Workington	13	54	11	11	89
Vauxhall	20	64	15	8	107
Dunlop	13	55	18	20	106
Mullard	17	53	15	11	96
	87	319	81	61	548

A modern kitchen, designed to make cooking as efficient and comfortable as possible for the modern woman – enabling her to be a worker as well as a housewife

He spoke to some of the men.

A turner said: "This is actually my idea not to have kids. The wife works full-time getting £6 a week as a grocer's assistant." A man of thirty-seven, married for nine years: "We can't afford at present to have children. My wife works full-time at Mullard getting £7 to £8 a week. We will have children later on." Another man of thirty-one, with a car and his own house, said: "My wife is on Staff, earning £11. She has no time for having a baby." Family planning seems to be one of the most important reasons for prosperity in the working classes, or at least it is so regarded by workers.

The Pill

The Family Planning Association runs 1000 clinics throughout Britain, giving advice to people to limit the number of children they have. In 1955 the work of this Association was helped by the discovery, in the USA, of the Pill. There were, and are, a number of different Pills produced by different drug firms; all of them have a common purpose—to prevent a woman having a baby. By 1970 over one and a half million women in Britain were taking one or other of the Pills.

The Pill received a great deal of publicity in 1968 when Pope Paul wrote a papal letter, *Humanae Vitae,* which condemned all forms of contraception, including the Pill.

A mothers and babies club where mothers meet to discuss problems

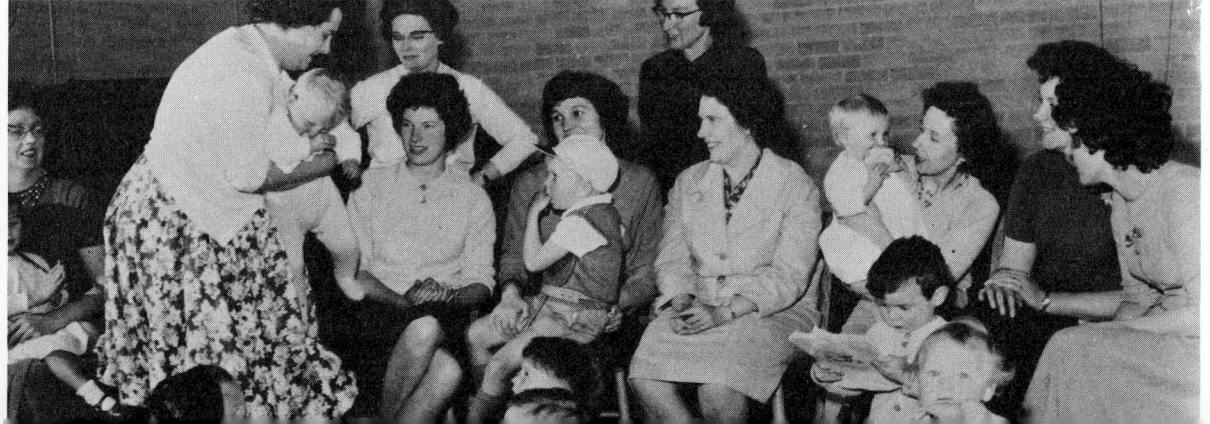

54,013 had abortions

A *Daily Telegraph* headline on abortion. Some people saw easy abortion as a sign of freedom, others as a sign of decadence

However, in 1970, the issue was clouded by a report that some forms of the Pill were dangerous to women's health and a number of Pills were taken off the market. In spite of Family Planning Association's various methods of contraception and the Pill, there was a continuing increase in the number of illegitimate births in England and Wales: 34,000 (4.8 per cent of the total number of live births) in 1956, and 63,000 (7.2 per cent of the total) in 1964. The figures for Scotland were 4,100 (4.3 per cent) and 5,600 (5.4 per cent); and for Northern Ireland 800 (2.7 per cent) and 1,000 (3 per cent). This means that one in fourteen babies born in the United Kingdom is illegitimate.

For mothers under twenty years the figures are far higher—about one in four of babies born are illegitimate. A particularly disturbing aspect of the situation is the youth of the girls who are conceiving outside marriage. Some of these marry before their children are born, and for those who marry in their teens the divorce rate is twice as high as for those who marry between twenty-one and twenty-four.

In 1961, 2,534 children were born to unmarried mothers aged between eleven and sixteen years old; over 4,100 children were born to unmarried mothers under the age of twenty. In the prosperous 1960s the figures became more alarming. In 1968 over 4,000 children were born to unmarried mothers under the age of sixteen and the number of illegal abortions had increased from about 50,000 in 1961 to about 100,000 in 1968.

This increase in the number of illegal abortions caused some medical men to support a Bill to allow legal abortions in certain circumstances. On 22 July 1966, the second reading was given to a Bill to legalize the medical termination of pregnancy in certain circumstances. The circumstances included danger to the health, physical or mental, of the pregnant woman; the risk that the child would be physically or mentally abnormal; the possibility that the pregnant woman's capacity as a mother would be severely overstrained by the care of another child.

In 1969 the Abortion Act became law, and since then women have been able to have abortions at private clinics or at National Health hospitals. There is some evidence that London has become the Abortion Capital for the world as women fly in from Europe and America to have their abortions here.

Cartoonist Horner's ironic view of the Pope's letter condemning contraception

'Suffer little children to come unto you.'

Chapter twenty-five
Crime and punishment

Before 1939 many people believed that the main causes of crime were slums, poverty and bad economic conditions. They hoped that following an improvement in general living standards, there would be no need for people to commit crime. Since 1945 Britain has had an almost continual improvement in living standards. Millions of new houses have been built, and thousands of acres of slums have been cleared. It is true that there are still many slum areas in our large cities, and many people who do not enjoy the fruits of the affluent society; but for the great majority of the people life in 1970 is much better, materially, than it was in the 1930s or 1940s.

And still the crime rate has continued to increase. A government report published in 1959 remarked: "It is a disquieting feature of our society that in the years since the War, rising standards in material prosperity, education and social welfare have brought no decrease in the high rate of crime; on the contrary, crime has increased and is still increasing."

Since 1945 there has been an annual average increase of 9 per cent in the number of crimes committed.

The general increase in crime is disturbing. Even more disturbing is the greater increase in the number of crimes committed by young people. One-third of all crimes are committed by people under the age of seventeen (which is twice the 1939 level) and one half of all the crimes committed in Britain are committed by people under the age of twenty-one (and this is three times the 1938 level). Another notable feature is that two-fifths of all crime comes under the general heading of "robbery with violence."

A photograph and headline in the *Daily Mirror* in 1970. The photograph is captioned: "The Police Move In"

The police

One reason for the increase in crime is that there are too few policemen; in 1965 the Home Secretary said that the country needed another 15,000 policemen if the police forces were to do

JUDGE IN DEMO COURT JAILS 14

Instant justice halts 'invasion'

A HIGH COURT judge handed out on-the-spot jail sentences to a band of young Welsh Nationalists who staged a dramatic invasion of his court yesterday.

Mr. Justice Lawton acted swiftly after one of the most astonishing protests ever seen in a British law court. He

Ban arms to Middle

Osbert Lancaster's cartoon showing young delinquents

their job properly. The shortage was, and is, greatest in London and the larger cities—where the crime rate is the highest. If there were more policemen about there might be fewer crimes committed, and there would be a greater chance of criminals being caught—which might deter other would-be criminals from breaking the Law.

In the nineteenth century, W. S. Gilbert wrote a song which had as its last line the words: "A policeman's lot is not a happy one." In the 1930s many people might have disagreed with this. The policeman had a secure job, a pension, good clothing and, more important, was popular with the vast majority of people. In the affluent 1960s policemen's wages were no better—indeed in many cases were worse—than wages earned by people doing much easier work with less demanding hours. In February 1965 a Home Office Report showed that the ordinary policeman earned £700 at nineteen, £1,000 at thirty, and the maximum of £1,100 was not reached until after twenty-two years service. Hours are long, (46 to 48 being a standard week), and irregular—including a good deal of shift and night work; conditions on the beat are lonely and often dangerous.

The criminal

One reason for the increase in crime is the motor car: criminals are more mobile. Before 1939 most policemen knew which people on their beat or in the area covered by their stations were likely to commit a certain type of crime. Today, criminals from London can commit a crime in Birmingham at 10.00 pm and be in their London beds by 2.00 am. In the late 1960s a gang of Australian shoplifters from Earl's Court, London, robbed shops in Cardiff, Bristol, Coventry and Manchester.

In the more affluent society there is more money around. Wage packets are higher—and criminals can make a rich haul if they attack a firm's cashier on his way back from the bank on pay-day. Shops take in more money—and criminals know that this has to be taken to a bank before the shop closes each night. Banks have more money on their premises than they used to have and are tempting prospects. Shoplifting is easier in the huge multiple stores than in the small shop of the 1930s.

The Great Train Robbery 1963

One of the twelve mail coaches that travelled regularly between Glasgow and London contained money for the London East Central Post Office. On the night of 8 August 1963, the train was stopped by a red signal just outside Cheddington. A team of thirty men disconnected the rear section and forced the driver to take the engine and the first two coaches forward half a mile. They then broke into the coach where banknotes were stacked in bags and stole over £2,500,000.

"The most disturbing feature of the whole case is that somewhere in the country there are still at large the men who gave the information about the best route, the best date, the load carried, the habits of the signalmen in the section eventually chosen. Someone warned the gang of a light load on the night of August 6/7, thereby altering the date of the robbery by 24 hours. Someone sent the final messages through from the North (one from Scotland, one from Carlisle)."

The criminals took their loot to a nearby farm, and but for a series of accidents might have got away with their crime.

Permissive society and crime

At different times since 1945 people have blamed different things for the increase in crime. At first they blamed the War, which broke up families, with the fathers in the Forces and the children evacuated: until the 1960s it could perhaps be said that most of the younger delinquents were war babies, and were perhaps the victims of under-feeding or of their parents' anxieties. Some blamed National Service, which took young people away at the age of eighteen. Bad schools, too much money, working mothers, over-indulgent parents, television, horror comics—all have been blamed for the growth of crime.

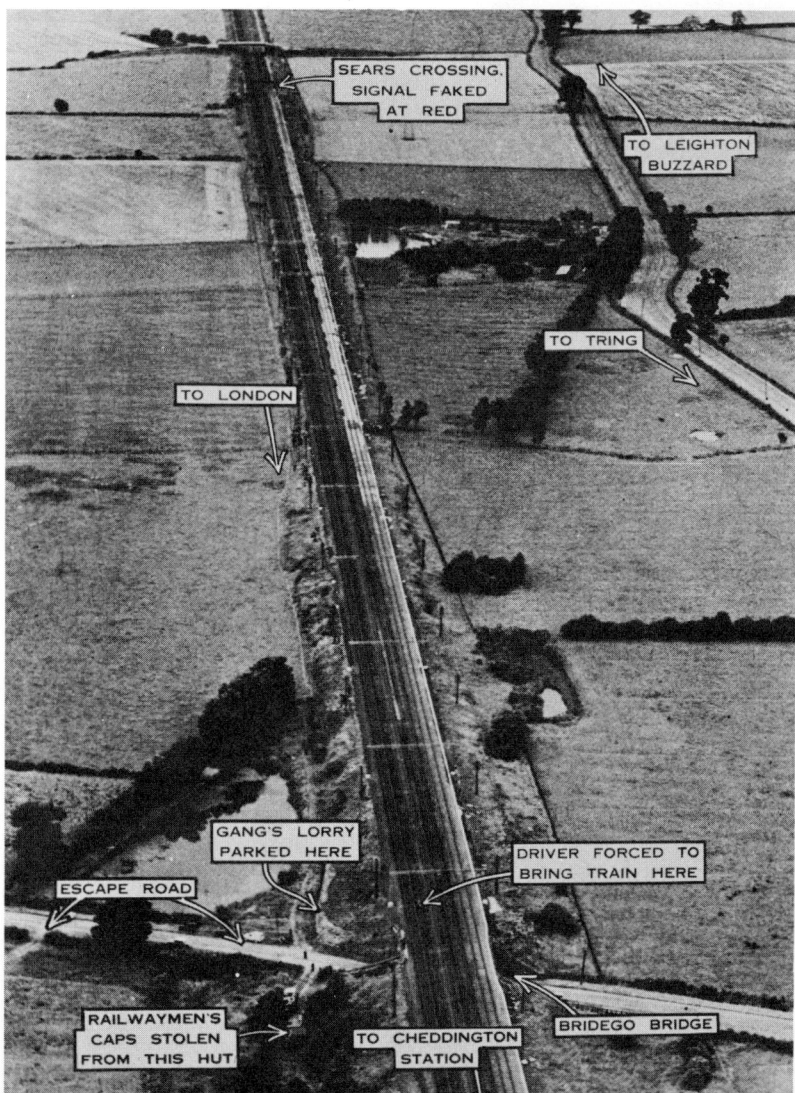

The scene of the Great Train Robbery

Derek Bentley's father and sister calling at the Home Office to plead for him

Morality and crime

In *Young Meteors* Jonathen Atiken quoted a teenage girl as saying: "If I see clothes I want and I can't afford them, I nick them. Yes, I nick them." She obviously did not think of herself as a criminal. Maurice Edelman, speaking in the House of Commons, said that young people were growing up in a society which regarded acquisition as the final end of life, and if they could not acquire legally then they turned to crime in order to get what they wanted. Fewer and fewer people believe that the criminal is to be blamed for his wrongdoing—the blame must lie elsewhere, with society, parents, television or advertising.

While the war against crime proper continues, there is a great deal of delinquency, largely on the part of the young, which is both vicious in itself and likely to lead to more serious crime. Trouble ranges from window-smashing to drugs; it includes wilful damage, brawling, gang fighting, sometimes the use of dangerous weapons.

Punishment—the death penalty

In 1948 the government abolished flogging as a punishment for criminals. During the debate on this the House of Lords rejected an amendment which would have abolished the death penalty for a trial period of five years.

In 1952 the Croydon police were called when two young men were seen trying to enter a warehouse. One of them, nineteen-year old Derek Bentley, was quickly captured and disarmed of his knife and knuckleduster. But he shouted "Give it to them, Chris," to his companion, Craig, who was armed with a rifle. Craig then killed a policeman, but because he was only sixteen he escaped hanging. Bentley was brought to trial as Craig's accomplice, and convicted of being an accessory to the murder, and sentenced to death. According to the *Daily Express* no execution had ever aroused such controversy: "In every pub and every club, in every home in the land the question is being discussed: 'Should Bentley hang?'"

He did hang; but many people were disturbed.

A Campaign for the Abolition of Capital Punishment was launched with Sidney Silverman as its spokesman in the House of Commons, and Victor Gollancz, the publisher, as one of its main propagandists outside Parliament. In 1955 a motion to abolish hanging was defeated in the Commons by 31 votes. In 1956 Ruth Ellis, a twenty-eight-year old mother of two children, was hung for shooting a faithless lover; in some countries this would have been called a crime of passion and she would not have been sentenced to death. In 1949 a mental defective, Timothy Evans, had been hung for the murder of his baby. The chief witness for the Crown was an ex-policeman, John Christie, who had been a lodger at Evans' house, 10 Rillington Place. In 1952 Christie was found guilty of the murder of six women whose bodies were buried in various parts of that house. Many people

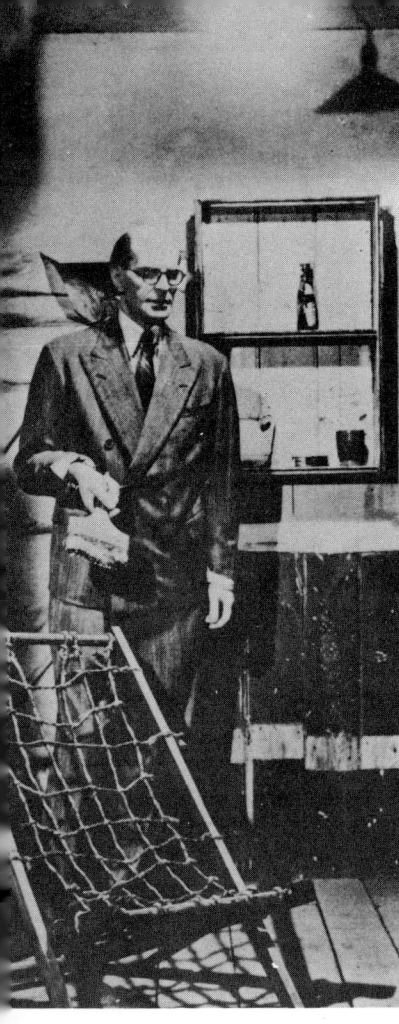

The wax model in Madame Tussaud's of John Christie

believed that Christie had murdered Evans' baby and that Evans had been wrongly convicted and hung.

Sidney Silverman's campaign reached a climax in 1956 when the House of Commons passed his Private Member's Bill, asking for abolition. The government was forced to take action, and in February 1957 brought in the Homicide Act, which abolished hanging for most crimes but retained it for others. This was obviously unsatisfactory. In 1965 the death sentence was abolished for a trial period of five years and in December 1969 this trial period was extended indefinitely. A future government may end this trial period and restore hanging; it seems unlikely.

Punishment—prison

The rebuilding and expansion of prisons lagged for some time behind the growth of crime—the total prison population numbered nearly 21,000 in 1956, 30,000 in 1964, an increase of 43 per cent. A massive building programme was planned which stepped up the amount spent in England and Wales from £822,000 in 1958–59 to nearly £7 million in 1964–65. New building, including the construction of more open prisons, at least one psychiatric prison, and re-equipment and conversion provided better facilities all round, making prison a place of constructive work with entertainment provided by films, concerts and by the prisoners themselves.

David and Ruth Ellis at Brand's Hatch

In August 1963 imprisonment for offenders under seventeen was abolished, and it is intended that eventually detention in a detention centre should replace short sentences of imprisonment for the seventeen-to-twenty-one age group. Public confidence was shaken by the escapes at different times and from different prisons of two long-term prisoners goaled for the notorious mail-train robbery of 1963. The murder of a young Borstal officer by escaping youths at the end of 1965 further shook public faith in official policy.

In March 1964 Government proposals for lump-sum monetary compensation for victims of crimes of violence became law. A Criminal Law Revision Committee, working alongside a general Law Reform Committee, was set up, while a Home Office Research Unit was formed for criminological research, and an Institute of Criminology was established at Cambridge with its own chair in Criminology.

In 1965 the Home Office summed up the position thus: "Research into the causes of crime and the effectiveness of the means of dealing with criminals is going ahead. The modernisation of the criminal law. . . is being pressed onward. The police service has been greatly strengthened and the enlarged Inspectorate and the new Police Research and Planning Branch at the Home Office will enhance police efficiency for the dual task of preventing crime and detecting offenders."

Backlash

In the USA public demand for action against criminals was greater in 1968 than at any previous time. Mr Nixon (then campaigning for the Presidency) promised to bring Law and Order to America's cities, and many people believe that this was a major reason for his success in that campaign. In February 1970 Mr Heath, and other Conservative leaders, issued an outline of the programme they would follow if they were returned to office at the next election. First on their list was a promise to restore Law and Order to British towns and cities. In this, as in much else, Britain has followed America's lead.

An aerial view of Pentonville Prison, London

Chapter twenty-six
A youthful society

From 1945 to 1960 Britain was recovering from the effects of the War, and building up the economic power which created—among other things—the affluent society. During this period people's attention was given to some of the older, more fundamental problems of an industrialised country—such as housing, the old and the sick, the development of new industries to replace the older, decaying industries, and to the acquisition by a large number of people of a higher standard of living. This period has been described as that of "the working-class man" because it was in this period that British working men first learned to enjoy the fruits of the affluent society and their wives learned how to spend increasing sums of money on themselves, their families and their homes.

Affluence and the teenager

It was not until 1959 that writers and manufacturers began to pay attention to the teenager. In 1959, the average male teenager spent 71s 6d a week, and the average girl 54s 0d. Britain's five million teenagers, after putting aside approximately £70 millions as true savings, spent £830 millions, or slightly over 5 per cent of the national total consumer expenditure. We have seen that the youthful invasion of the fashion scene began in 1958, when Mary Quant produced her first designs. Youthful entertainers like the Beatles became prominent at about the same time. In 1964 Harold Wilson became the youngest Prime Minister of the century and one of the measures passed by his government was to lower the voting age to eighteen—as if acknowledging that youth had come of age.

Piccadilly Circus is a popular gathering place for young people from all over the world. In spite of the traffic, they gather there to talk, watch, and even play records

Skinheads in their "uniform": tight jeans, usually with braces, large boots and cropped hair

Students on grants joined the working teenagers in creating a demand for clothes, entertainment and more manufactured products. This economic revolution was catered for by the commercial enterprises which know that a sizeable proportion of the national income goes into the pockets of young earners. As a result, teenagers have been transformed into a highly self-conscious stratum in society.

The Britisher teenager is better fed, healthier and richer than his parents were. He is also more mature physically now that puberty begins six months earlier with each generation. This is a major reason for the increased attention paid to sex, although another reason is what David Holbrook calls a "completely packaged Brave New World of sexual awareness, from commercial sources." T. R. Fyvel agrees that "sex has never received such massive publicity as today, from the ubiquitous under-clothes advertisements to the incessant erotic gossip in the popular press."

Neither fan clubs nor pop stars are the creation of the modern teenager. Bing Crosby and others were idolised in the 1930s, and Johnny Ray's appearances caused riots in the 1950s. What is new is that the pop stars tend to be much younger now than they were in the 1930s or 1950s, and they are supported by much larger numbers of fans. In part this is the result of affluence; young people can afford to spend a weekend on the Isle of Wight at a Bob Dylan happening; in the 1930s they would not have had the money to do so. In part it is also the result of greater freedom; some modern teenagers think little of sleeping away from home for days at a time.

Working-class teenagers

The provision of more higher education and the development of new industries have opened up a number of ways in which young people can "get on." Thirty per cent of the university population comes from the working class—although this still means that a child of manual labouring parents has much less chance of going to university than the child of middle-class parents. These working-class children who go to university or colleges, or who get promotion through apprenticeship schemes, become members of the middle class, buying all the symbols of their new class—the car, the holiday abroad, the clothes and furniture.

However, there are very many working-class children who realise at fifteen or sixteen that they are not going to get on at all. They realise that they have no formal qualifications nor have they the basic education to allow them to become qualified through work at a night school or a day release class. They work as unskilled labourers and know that they have little, if any, hope of rising above this level. Some of these children become "Skinheads," forming their own gangs to show their resentment against society in a violent way. They have their own style of dress, their own language and code of conduct. Their maturity, affluence and freedom join together to produce a violent society which causes Quintin Hogg—Conservative Party spokesman on Law—to say that the permissive society is a lawless society.

Middle-class teenagers

Middle-class children have a better chance of getting higher education. Most of them, like their working-class colleagues and their parents, take advantage of the opportunity to become qualified so that they too can join in the acquisitive race of the affluent society. Some of them, however, believe that the race is not worthwhile; they believe that the mere acquisition of more material goods is not what life should be about. An increasing number of these middle-class children try to reject society and the world around them and enter the dream world of Zen Buddhism or some other exotic religious sect; they, too, like the Skinheads, have their own uniform or dress, behaviour, language and code of conduct. They become the Hippies and the Yippies, among whom drug-taking is commonplace.

Hippies in London

Revolution

Other of the more educated, mature and affluent children who are critical of our society have decided that they want to play an active part in changing some of society's ideas and practices. Students at the London School of Economics rioted in 1968 in protest against the appointment of a new Principal; they disliked the part he had played as Principal of the University of Southern Rhodesia and decided that they didn't want him in LSE. Having lost that battle, they demanded greater student participation in the governing of the School, in the appointment of staff and in the decisions as to what they should study. Their example was taken up by students in other places; the Colleges of Art at Guildford and Hornsey were closed for months because of student demonstrations; in 1970 sit-ins at the Universities of Birmingham and Sussex were followed by similar demonstrations at Oxford, Cambridge, Warwick and other universities.

These students are politically active. They oppose American policy in Vietnam, apartheid in South Africa, British policy in Nigeria, the racialist policies of Enoch Powell. Student leaders helped to organise Catholic protest in Northern Ireland in 1968, and one of their leaders, Bernadette Devlin, was later elected MP for Mid-Ulster, the youngest woman ever to be elected.

It is fitting, perhaps, that at a time when youth dominates the scene the Royal Family should be represented by two young people. Prince Charles, since his investiture as the Prince of Wales, shows every sign of being more informal and "with it" than previous Princes were allowed to be. Princess Anne, who has blossomed into an attractive young woman, shares the tastes of many of her age group.

The Queen, the Duke of Edinburgh and Prince Charles just after the latter's Investiture as Prince of Wales

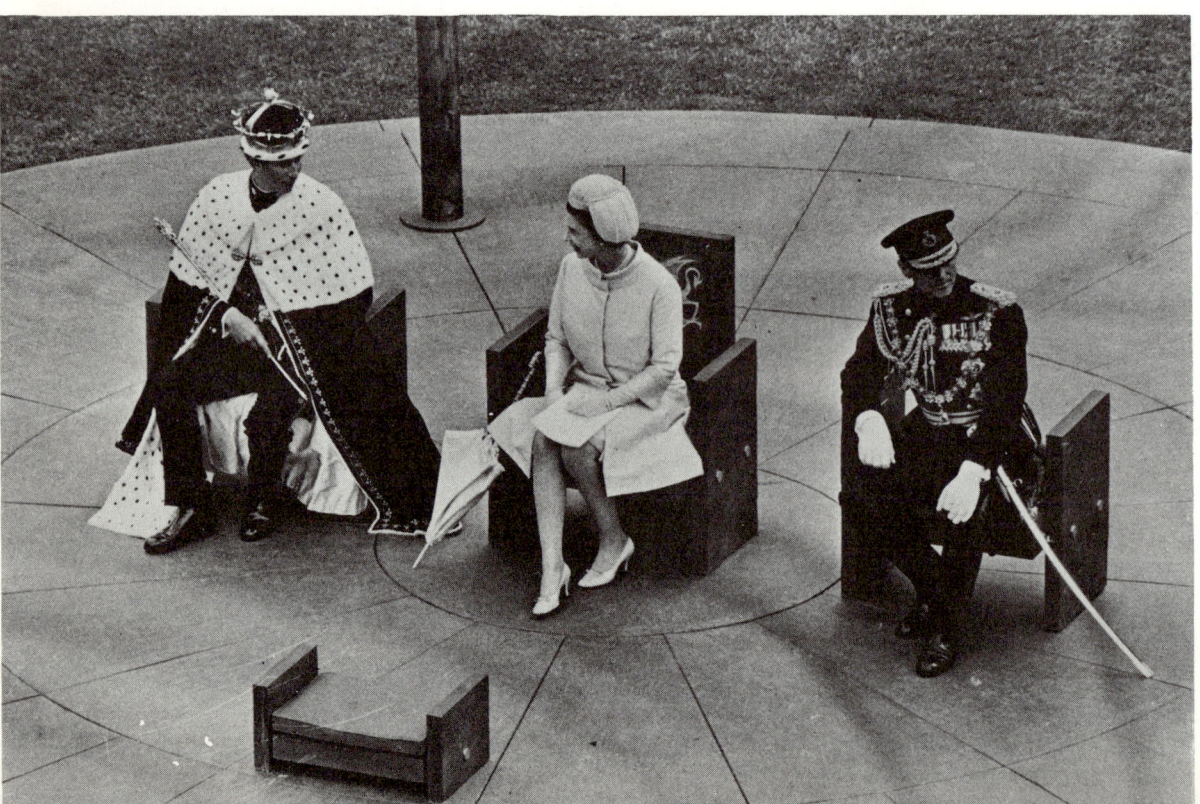

Chapter twenty-seven
Pop music

A more affluent public was able to spend more money on entertainment in general [Chapter 21] in the mid-1950s. One of the ways in which they spent this money was on records made by dance bands—led by popular leaders such as Ted Heath, Cyril Stapleton, Joe Loss or by singers such as Donald Peers and Vera Lynn.

Tommy Steele

In 1956, Tommy Hicks—a nineteen year old ex-cabin boy who played a guitar and sang with a Cockney accent—was launched into show business and achieved fame so rapidly that within a year he was working on his film biography—*The Tommy Steele Story*. His first song hit, *Singing the Blues*, made his name a household word—Britain's answer to the young American star Elvis Presley.

Tommy Steele was the first in a long line of young pop singers and his success inspired the formation of a number of guitar-playing groups. For a time these groups were known as "skiffle groups" and thousands of people, even the very young, joined in this craze—which died after a brief lifetime. Guitar-playing groups and individual guitar-playing singers remained; they were popular with young people who went to newly-opened clubs to hear the latest group.

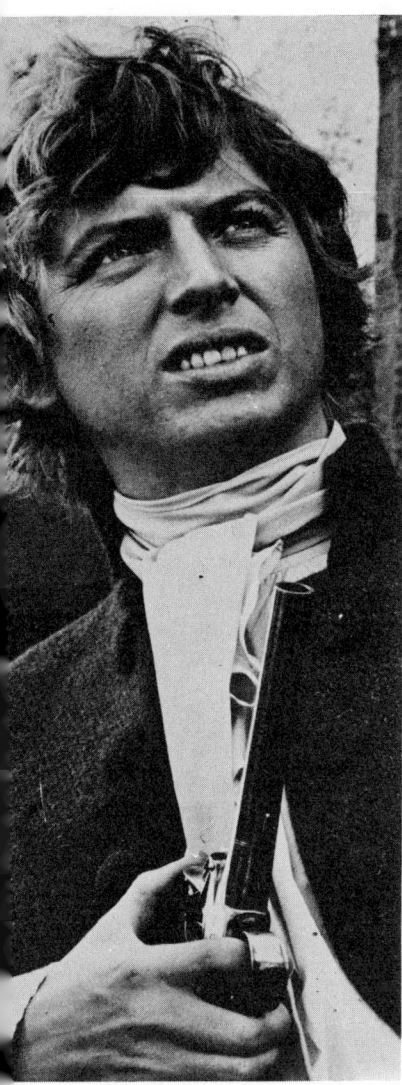

Tommy Steele as he appears in *Where's Jack?*

The craze for skiffle did not last long, but it was very intense while it did last

Pop idols of the 70s receive much the same treatment from their fans as the first idols. Here Bill Haley, King of Rock 'n' Roll, is seen arriving from America in 1957. He was met by hundreds of screaming teenagers who pushed police aside and forced Haley's car to stop. Police climbed on to the car roof to fight off the fans

The Beatles

In 1963 one of the many groups became outstandingly popular, so much so that one writer has said: "1963 was the year of the Beatles." A *Time* magazine report of 21 February 1964 said: "Adults may not dig, but how could 20 million teenagers be wrong? The Beatles are fab. The Beatles are great. The Beatles are cool, cool, cool, cool, ... They are pure and classic idols. All they have to do is lift their arms or shake their waterweed hair to provoke screams that would block out an all-clear signal. Fans scream so steadily through each song that they cannot possibly hear what is being sung.

But the Beatles are really Teddy bears, covered over with Piltdown hair. The one word that teenagers use to describe them is 'different.' They are different not only because they all grope around under four years' growth of hair. They are different because they are as wholesome as choir boys.

What recommends the Beatles more than anything else is their bright and highly irreverent attitude towards themselves: 'Why do you wear so many rings, Ringo?' ... 'Because I can't fit them all through my nose.' 'What do you think of Beethoven, Ringo?' ... 'I love his poems.' "

The Beatles' fame soon spread to the USA, where they had more fans than they had in Britain; by 1965 they had sold over 225 million records and had been awarded the MBE "for services to British exports." British pop stars such as the Beatles and the Rolling Stones, became international stars; they were imitated by singers and groups in the USA and Europe and the youthful musical revolution was an international one.

The international scene

Pop stars flew in and out of various continents. While Bob Dylan's fans assembled in the half million on the Isle of Wight, Britain's Rolling Stones were attracting similar audiences in Australia and were planning to go on to the USA. Idolisation of stars is not new. Bing Crosby, Frank Sinatra and Johnny Ray all had their mass following in the 1940s and 1950s. The new stars are younger than the others—partly in response to the emergence of the affluent teenager, partly because of the general tendency to youthfulness in society in general.

The new idols differ from their predecessors in that they do not accept the conventions of existing society. Crosby, Sinatra and Ray dressed and looked like other members of society. The young pop artists do not try to look like the older, conventional, ordinary members of society. Their hair styles, dress, behaviour—on and off the stage—is an attack on older, more conventional ideas. Their songs are often songs of protest against society, or of attack on some idea (such as marriage) which society believes in. In this case the pop groups may be seen either as just a part of the youthful revolution, or they may be seen as leaders of that revolution.

Most of the young pop stars are male; a few girls—Sandie Shaw, Dusty Springfield and Cilla Black—have become as famous as

Bob Dylan singing to the crowds at the Isle of Wight Pop Festival in 1969. He was paid £38,000 and sang for one hour

The Beatles as they were once – together

the Beatles, Gerry and the Pacemakers, Peter and Gordon and other boys. Even these few girls have become famous without exploiting their sex, unlike previous popular female stars. To older listeners all pop groups seem alike; to the young there are square and "in" groups. Once the Beatles were the "in" group; as they became more popular with older people, were decorated and interviewed by the Prime Minister and Church leaders, so they became less popular with the young who adopted the Rolling Stones as their idols.

The classless group

One of the essential features of the pop scene is that it is dominated by groups and not by individuals. In the 1940s and 1950s the popular music scene was dominated by bands under the control of an individual—Heath, Loss, Stapleton, Billy Cotton and so on. Modern pop music owes very little to individuals; there are few groups which are dominated by an individual such as Gerry and the Pacemakers and the young know that these groups tend to be the "squarer" groups.

Another feature of the pop scene is that it is a classless one. Peter and Gordon were boys from Westminster School; their music was enjoyed by millions of young people of every class and with differing educational backgrounds.

Records

Older people sometimes think that the young are exploited by recording companies and their agents. They think that the companies pick which groups are to develop, which records are to get into the best-selling charts. The recording companies wish that this were true; it would save them the trouble and expense of pressing off hundreds of new records each week and the effort to promote each of them. It is the record-buying teen-agers who decide what will be a "hit" or a "miss" and not a panel

Pop star Cilla Black at her wedding to her road manager, Bobby Willis, in 1969

of experts—even teenage experts.

In March 1970 the sound track from Lee Marvin's *Paint your Waggon* became the best-selling record—although it is merely the sound of a drunkard singing his way home. No company or panel of experts could have forecast that this is what the teenagers would buy.

Most of the records are made by two companies—EMI (the larger of the two), and Decca. They press over eighty-five of every hundred British-made records. They are at the centre of a new industry which has grown as a result of teenage demand. Records have to be made in studios, promoted by advertisement, sold in shops and commented on in newspapers. Records are played in discotheques, in coffee bars and public houses; groups appear in one-night shows at dance halls up and down the country, as well as appearing overseas. Their appearances have to be arranged, advertised and organised—another part of the pop world.

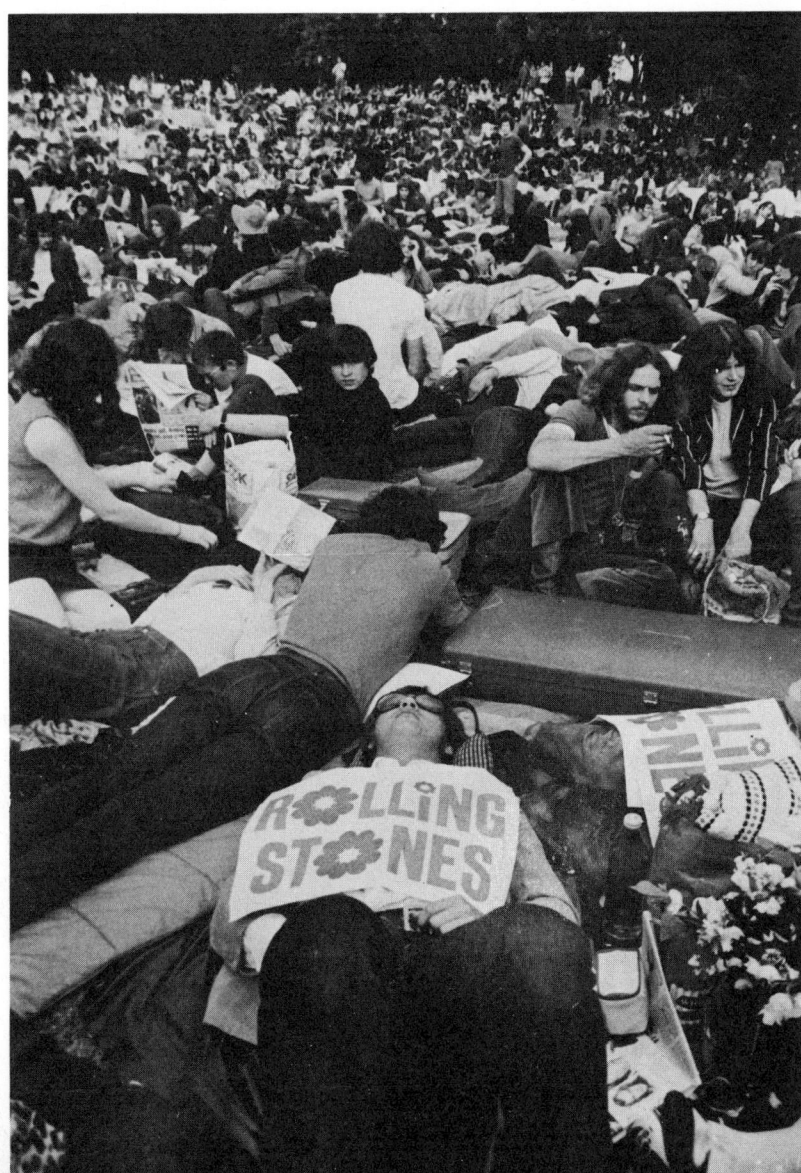

The Rolling Stones were among the most popular groups of the middle and late sixties. Here, about half a million fans wait for them to appear at the Stones' largest ever outdoor concert in Hyde Park in 1969

Chapter twenty-eight
The permissive society

One of the main features of life in post-War Britain has been the removal of a number of restrictions on people's freedom—to read what they like, to see what films and plays they like and to behave as they like—without interference from policemen, censors or other authority.

Americanisation

Some people think that this greater freedom is due to the Americanisation of the British way of life. In *The New Look*, Harry Hopkins wrote: "From hula-hoops to Zen Buddhism, from do-it-yourself to launderettes or the latest sociological catch-phrase or typographical trick, from Rock 'n' Roll to Action Painting, barbecued chickens rotating on their spits in the shop windows to parking meters, clearways, bowling alleys, glass skyscrapers, flying saucers, pay-roll raids, armoured trucks and beatniks, American habits and vogues now crossed the Atlantic with a speed and certainty that suggested that Britain was now merely one more off-shore island. Striptease clubs completed the "Fordisation" of sex, supermarkets of shopping and Wimpy bars of eating. As if by some automatic process every successful American stereo or gimmick duly appeared in British version—a Dors for a Monroe, a Steele for a Presley, a Shirley Bassey for an Eartha Kitt. The freeing of Lawrence's Lady Chatterley which took place in Britain in 1960 was preceded by her liberation in the United States in 1959. American drug-houses furnished our tranquilisers, American publishers our excitement with the co-operation of British publishers who found the recommendation 'sweeping the US' ever more compulsive. A second Canadian financier now continued the Americanization of our Press which the first had some time before begun. And there was still an American musical on the boards of Dury Lane in the expert packaging of *My Fair Lady*."

The Wolfenden Report

However, in at least one respect, Britain was running ahead of America.

The Wolfenden Report was published in September 1957. It represented three years' work by a committee set up under the chairmanship of the vice-chancellor of Reading University, Sir John Wolfenden, to examine "the whole law and practice relating to homosexual offences and prostitution." The chief recommendation was a change in the law making homosexual acts between consenting adults in private no longer illegal. According to the opinion polls the public were fairly evenly divided on the ques-

Sir John Wolfenden, who led the Departmental Committee on Homosexual Offences and Prostitution 1954-57, which produced the Wolfenden Report

Permissiveness and clothes means that you can wear exactly what you like when and where you like. Here Josje Leeger wears clothes of her own design, which pile layer upon layer of exotically shaped garments upon one another

tion but most of the newspapers declared in favour of the reform. As usual the *Daily Mirror* offered the most outspoken comment. It's readers were told: "Don't be Shocked by this Report. It's the Truth. It's the Answer. IT'S LIFE."

Publishing

In 1960 the government tried to persuade the Penguin Press not to publish *Lady Chatterley's Lover*; when Allen Lane insisted on doing so the government prosecuted the firm, who won their case and established their right to publish this book. We have already seen that *La Dolce Vita* was a film which shocked the world in 1960, although compared to films produced and shown since, it is a fairly harmless story. Similarly, in 1960, *Lady Chatterley's Lover* was attacked by some people as a filthy, depraved book, while others thought that Allen Lane's decision to publish the book was a major step along the road to freedom. Other publishers have taken advantage of this freedom to publish books which make *Lady Chatterley's Lover* look like a mild fairy story.

Writers, playwrights and film producers portrayed sex as a social problem (e.g. in *Up the Junction*), while others took advantage of the newly-won freedom to produce near-pornographic films.

Some people think that 1969 was the year of the permissive society. Nudity on films became commonplace and lesbianism was allowed on the screen. A boom market for sex comics was created in New York and in Denmark censorship on films and books was totally abandoned. In New York, Kenneth Tynan produced *Oh, Calcutta!* [Chapter 21]. In London an American company produced *Hair*.

In Britain, gambling was legalised in 1963 and by 1968 there were over 1,000 gambling casinos. Divorce was made progressively easier, and in 1970 Parliament approved of divorce by consent. Homosexuality is no longer a crime and the Abortion Law allows people to get rid of unwanted babies.

Gambling in a casino

Police assaulted as 40 youths run amok in High-street

TWO 18-YEARS-OLD Carshalton youths were sent to a detention centre for three months when they were found guilty at Sutton court last week of assaulting PC Colin Meakin while in the execution of his duty outside the Wimpey Bar in High-street, Sutton.

This headline from the *Carshalton Times* indicates another, less pleasant side to the "civilised" society of the 70s

Civilised society

Roy Jenkins, formerly Home Secretary in the Labour government, claimed some of the credit for the relaxing of many British laws. He argued that the permissive society was a civilised society. Certainly it was a less hypocritical society than that of, say, Victorian Britain, where people paraded their religion on Sunday, only to ill-treat workpeople during the week, and where crime, violence, promiscuity and prostitution were "ignored" as if swept under the carpet. Certainly it seems civilised to allow adult people to make up their own minds as to how they will spend their money rather than having a government forbidding them to gamble, and freedom to read what they like and to see what films and plays they like. In this sense the permissive society has encouraged people to "do their own thing" and Britain in the 1970s is more alive than it was in the 1950s. It is also a kinder society, caring for the old, the deprived, the homeless, the victims of war in a way that was not evident in the 1930s. People are not hounded because they do not conform to a set pattern; homosexuals, lesbians, long-haired and short-haired, thrusting industrialists and sit-around pop guitarists are tolerated in this freer society.

Vandalism has grown alongside "civilisation." Here is the inside of a train wrecked by football crowds

Roy Jenkins, to whom goes some of the credit for making some British laws less rigid

"Flower people" speaking at Hyde Park Corner for the legislation of cannabis

Immoral society

However, it would be foolish to pretend that this is the whole story. In this freer society there is a continuing increase in the rate of illegitimacy and of venereal disease among young people who have not learned to use their freedom wisely. There is a continuing increase in the numbers of young people taking drugs, such as heroin; it seems that freedom creates problems for young people who are not able to deal with them, and who try to escape from reality into the dream drug world. There is a continuing increase in hooliganism—on trains, in the streets, at football matches, on the beaches and in dance halls. The civilised, permissive society is the result of an attack on authority, on the laws which prevent people being free. Now that these laws have been removed there are fewer people who have any idea of "right" or "wrong;" fewer adults willing to take a moral stand on moral problems, so that the young have also been given their freedom. They seem incapable of distinguishing between their freedom to do what they like, and the effect of their actions on the freedom of other people (to travel by train, to go to a game, to enjoy a day at the seaside).

Chapter twenty-nine
Summing-up

Britain has now passed through twenty-five post-War years and experienced many changes in economic, social and intellectual life. Indeed, it is doubtful if there has ever been another period in which so much changed in so short a time. In 1970 the government owns large sections of industry, and controls other, larger sections through the work of the Ministry of Technology, the Department of Employment and Productivity and the Prices and Incomes Board. It spends vast sums of money on the welfare of the British people, who are better fed, educated and housed, healthier and live longer to enjoy a more affluent life than ever before. An ever-increasing number of young people are going on to some form of further education after the age of fifteen, so that already there are too few colleges and universities to cater for all those who wish to enter.

In the same period Britain has lost an Empire and her leadership of the free world. The British people also seemed to have given up the morality of the past. In *Honest to God* the Bishop of Woolwich, Dr Robinson, said that while Victorians such as Darwin and Huxley had attacked the doctrines of Christianity, their grandchildren seemed to have rejected Christian morality. There is now less idea of "right" and "wrong" than there used to be.

Members of the Welsh Freedom Army in training in Wales

The white eagle of Snowdon, emblem of the Welsh Freedom Army

Londoners in a clash with the police in 1963

These changes have determined the spirit of the age. The power of government has grown and industrial firms have become larger; someone, somewhere makes decisions affecting the lives of millions of people. Some people have resented this and have begun to demand a share in that decision-making. In one case this has led to the call for separate governments for Scotland and Wales; in another to the demand for worker participation in industrial decision-making and trade unionists have asked for a seat on the boards of management.

This demand for "participation" has been most forcibly expressed by university students. They have demanded, and obtained, a share in the government of the universities. They now sit with teachers, deciding what should be taught and how they should be examined. When they suspect that the university authorities are acting in "an old-fasioned, high-handed way" the students try to force them to change policies. They strike, take over the university buildings so that work is held up, search through files and records to see what, if anything, has been noted about individual students. This is a far cry from the peace and quiet of a seat of learning which universities seem to have been in the past.

In the past the British people grumbled about "them"—meaning the government, employers and authority in general. In the 1920s and 1930s the unemployed marched to London to protest against the government's failure to help them. But such protests had little effect. In post-War Britain, protest has been more forceful and effective. The first important protest movement was the Campaign for Nuclear Disarmament (CND). One of its leaders was the philosopher, Bertrand Russell. In April 1961 he said: "We used to call Hitler wicked for killing off the Jews, but Kennedy and Macmillan are much more wicked than Hitler. We cannot obey the murderers. They are wicked. They are abominable. They are the wickedest people who have ever lived in the history of man and it is our duty to do what we can against them. This idea of weapons of mass destruction is utterly horrible and is something with which no one with one spark of humanity can tolerate. I will not pretend to obey a government which is organizing a mass massacre of mankind. I will do everything I can to oppose the government in every way which I feel will be fruitful. I exhort you to do the same."

By 1961 the CND movement had attracted a good deal of attention and support through its annual Easter march from the Aldermaston Atomic Weapon Research Establishment to Trafalgar Square. The first of these was held in 1958 when 50,000 supporters joined the march. In 1960 over 100,000 people marched to try to persuade the government to abandon the nuclear bomb.

This campaign began because some people wanted to influence government. They also wanted to make the present and the future better for other people. This is another feature of post-War society—it has been a "caring" society. Some people have campaigned actively for better housing, and have supported the Shelter campaign begun by a young New Zealander, Des Wilson. Others have supported Oxfam and similar organisations trying to improve the lives of people in under-developed countries. Campaigns to help the poor, the old, the handicapped, the sick and other less-well-off members of society have been actively

Above and on the right: children at school in the 70s. The future depends largely on them

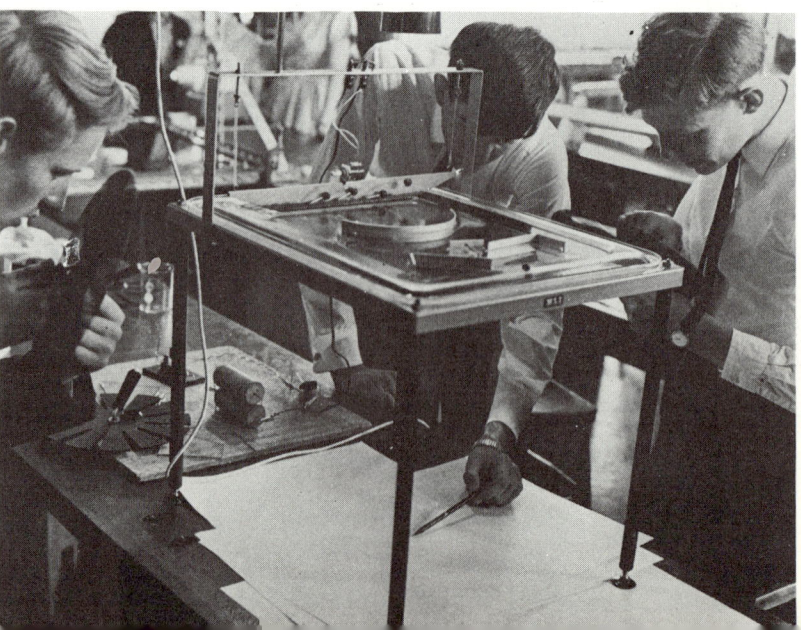

supported and have caused government policy to change.

Some people believe that this desire for participation, change and action should be resisted. They believe that authority has the right to tell students what to do, that movements such as CND and Anti-Apartheid should be stopped. Others agree with Beveridge who said that the Welfare State would make people more secure, confident and demanding than they had been [Chapter 3]. They believe that the demand for participation is yet another proof that post-War Britain is a freer, better Britain.

Roy Jenkins, formerly Home Secretary in the Wilson government, has called it a "civilised society" which has given people more freedom to lead their own lives in their own way. On the other hand, many people fear that the increasingly free and permissive society is in danger of becoming a violent, destructive and evil society. They would agree with Sir Kenneth Clark the art historian who said, in 1969: "one . . . may be optimistic but one can't be joyful at the prospect before us." He quoted a poem written fifty years ago by W. B. Yeats:

> Things fall apart; the centre cannot hold;
> Mere anarchy is loosed upon the world,
> The blood-dimmed tide is loosed, and everywhere
> The ceremony of innocence is drowned:
> The best lack all conviction, while the worst
> Are full of passionate intensity.

Roy Jenkins is one of the optimists who believe that society will get better as man gets used to using his freedom. Sir Kenneth Clark is one of the pessimists who think that freedom may degenerate into licence. The next twenty-five years of life in post-War Britain will prove which of them is correct. These children will know the answer.

Children marching for *Shelter*, **the organisation which tries to tackle the problem of the homeless**

Some suggestions for further reading

1 General surveys of the post-War period
The New Look (on the 40s and 50s) by Harry Hopkins, Secker & Warburg
The New Classes (on the affluent society) by R. Millar, Longmans
The Changing Social Structure of England and Wales, 1871-1951 by David Marsh, Routledge 1958
Social Mobility in Britain by D. V. Glass (ed.), Routledge 1956
British Economic Policy Since the War by Andrew Shonfield, Penguin 1958

2 Detailed studies of shorter periods
The British General Election of 1950 by H. G. Nicholas, Macmillan
The British General Election of 1951 by D. E. Butler, Macmillan
The British General Election of 1955 by D. E. Butler, Macmillan
The British General Election of 1959 by D. E. Butler and R. Rose, Macmillan
The British General Election of 1964 by D. E. Butler and A. King, Macmillan
The British General Election of 1966 by D. E. Butler and A. King, Macmillan
Each volume has a survey of the period prior to the election and an examination of the main issues of the time, as well as some good illustrations.
The Uproarious Years by Cummings, MacGibbon & Kee 1954
Low Visibility, a Cartoon History 1945-53 by David Low, Collins 1953
The Fearful Fifties by David Low, Bodley Head 1960
Labour's First Year by J. E. D. Hall, Penguin 1947
The Britain We Saw by Herbert and Nancy Matthews, Gollancz 1950
The Forties by Alan Ross, Weidenfeld & Nicolson 1950
The Fifties by J. Montgomery, Weidenfeld & Nicolson
The Age of Austerity (1945-50 as remembered by young people) M. Sissons and P. French (eds.) Hodder & Stoughton

3 Examinations of particular topics

Britain in the 60s a series of Penguin Specials which deals with most of the topical issues—*Housing* by S. Alderson, *The Family* by R. Fletcher, *The Future of the Welfare State* by D. C. Marsh are outstanding
Anger and After (on the theatre) by J. R. Taylor, Penguin
The Insecure Offenders (on delinquents) by T. R. Flyvel, Chatto & Windus
Scandal '63 (on the Profumo affair) by C. Irving et alia, Heinemann
The Suez Crisis by Paul Johnson, Penguin
The Beatles' Progress (on pop music) by M. Braun, Penguin
The Young Meteors (on youthful society) by J. Aitken, Secker & Warburg
The Neophiliacs (on cultural/moral decline) by C. Booker, Collins
Beveridge and His Plan by Janet Beveridge, Hodder & Stoughton
Soccer Nemesis by Brian Glanville, Secker & Warburg 1955
The Newcomers by Ruth Glass, Allen & Unwin 1960
The Story of the Lynskey Tribunal by Wilfred March, Redman 1949
Poverty and the Welfare State by B. S. Rowntree & G. R. Lavers, Longmans 1951
The British Worker by Ferdynand Zweig, Penguin 1952
The Worker in the Affluent Society by Ferdynand Zweig, Heinemann 1961
Essays on the Welfare State by Richard Titmuss, Allen & Unwin 1958
Social Class and Education Opportunity by Floud, Halsey & Martin, Heinemann 1956
Inside the Comprehensive School (Symposium) Schoolmaster Pub. Co. 1958
Comprehensive Education by Robin Pedley, Gollancz 1956
Divorce in England by O. R. McGregor, Heinemann 1957
Obscenity and the Law by N. St. J. Stevas, Secker & Warburg 1956
Dior by Dior by Christian Dior, Weidenfeld & Nicolson 1957
Women's Two Roles: Home and Work by A. Myrdal and V. Klein, Routledge 1956
The Angry Decade by Kenneth Allsop, Owen 1958
The Big Beat Scene by Royston Ellis, Four Square 1961
The Uses of Literacy by Richard Hoggart, Chatto 1957
Television in Britain P.E.P. 1958
Pressure Groups, the Campaign for Commercial Television by H. H. Wilson, Secker & Warburg 1961

4 Individual memoirs or biographies

Frank Cousins by Margaret Stewart, Heinemann
Macmillan by Anthony Sampson, Allen Lane, the Penguin Press
The Other Side of the Hill (on N.H.S.) by Charles Hill, Heinemann
Quant on Quant by Mary Quant, Cassell

The Making of the Prime Minister by A. Howard and R. West, Chatto & Windus
The Greasy Pole by R. Bevins, Hodder & Stoughton
As it Happened by C. R. Attlee, Heinemann 1954
A Prime Minister Remembers by C. R. Attlee and Francis Williams, Heinemann 1961
I Fight to Live by Robert Boothby, Gollancz 1947
High Tide and After by Hugh Dalton, Muller 1962
Autobiography by Herbert Morrison, Odhams 1960
Memoirs by Lord Woolton, Cassell 1959
Fifty Tumultuous Years by Earl Winterton, Hutchinson 1955
Along my Line by Gilbert Harding, Putnam 1953
Tommy Steele by John Kennedy, Souvenir Press 1958

Index

Abadan 32–33, 81
Abbey Steelworks, Port Talbot 15, 26, 68, 92
abolition of capital punishment 134
abortion 130, 147
Adenauer, Dr 70, 75
Admiralty 109
advertising 62, 104–107, 118
affluence 25–26, 90, 104–107, 117–118, 122, 124, 138–139
affluent society 27, 50–51, 56, 58, 62–63, 66, 70, 93, 104–111, 125–126, 131–132, 137, 139, 141, 143
Africa 81–86, 93, 120
aircraft design 107
aircraft engines 107
aircraft industry 17, 57, 108
airline companies 106–108
airports 107
air travel 107–108
Akaba, Gulf of 83
Aldermaston 152
Algerian rebels 83
America (USA) 38–41, 47, 49, 76, 80–86, 100, 140
Americanisation 120, 146
Angry Young Men 63, 114
Anne, Princess 140
apartheid 117, 140, 153
Arabs 31
Archers, the 104
Arts Council 115
Arts, Ministry of 115
Asia 86, 93
Assistance Board 20
Assistance, National 18, 20
Aswan High Dam 82
atomic bomb 42–43
Atomic Energy Authority 76
Attlee, Clement (Lord) 8, 12, 16, 30, 32–34, 36, 41, 43, 45–47, 50, 84
Australia 29, 78, 94

balance of payments 68, 70, 74, 119–120
bankers, foreign 68
Bank of England 13
Bank Rate 13
Bannister, Roger 115–116
Battersea 37, 66
BBC 13, 50–51, 104, 106–107
Beatles 142–144
Beckett, Samuel 114
Beeching, Dr Reginald 110
Belgium 77
Beloff, Norah 77
Bentley, Derek 134
Berlin 40–41
Berlin Airlift 41
Betting and Gaming Act 113
Bevan, Aneurin 20–21, 46–47, 54, 64
Beveridge Report 19, 24, 52, 87, 98
Bevin, Ernest 8, 10, 33, 45, 58, 62, 77, 87
bingo 113
Birch, Nigel 64
Birmingham 97, 111, 132, 140
Black, Cilla 143–144
Blackpool 119
BOAC 13, 51, 109
Board of Trade 28, 66, 77, 122
Boeing 108
Bombay 31
bomb damage 8–9, 54
Boothby, Sir Robert 23
borrowing abroad 8–9, 68, 70–71, 81

borstal 136
Bowden, Lord 100
Boyle, Sir Edward 103
Braddock, Bessie 93
Brasher, Christopher 116
bread rationing 34–36
Brighton 100
Bristol 115
British Railways 72, 89, 110
Brown, George 46, 69, 80, 89–90
Butler, David 53
Butler, R. A. 22, 48, 50, 73, 98
Butlin, Sir Billy 118–119

Cairo 33
Callaghan, James 68
Cambridge University 136, 140
camping 118–119
Canada 29, 78, 94
Canterbury 100
capital punishment 134
caravans 119
Carnaby Street 123
cars 110
Castle, Barbara 127–128
CATs 100–101
Celtic FC 116
Central Electricity Generating Board 13, 17, 71, 90
Chamberlain, Neville 81, 87
Charles, Prince of Wales 140
Chataway, Christopher 115–116
chemical industry 57
Chetwynd, Mrs H. R. 102
children 98–103, 152·153
China 42–43
Christie, John 134–135
Churchill, Sir Winston 7, 39, 47–48, 50, 77, 85, 87, 98–99
cinema 112–113
Civil Servants 91, 126
Clark, Sir Kenneth 153
classless society 60–64, 66, 98, 103, 123, 144
clothes-rationing 36, 111, 122
CND 66, 152
Coal Acts 13–14
Coal Board 13–14, 28
coal industry 57
coal—nationalisation 9–14
Coal and Steel Community 77
Cockerell, Christopher 109
Colchester 100–101
Colleges of Advanced Technology 100–101
coloured children 95–97
coloured headmistress 94
coloured immigrants and workers 93–97
colour supplements 107
Common Market 66, 70–77, 80
Commonwealth—food 78
Commonwealth Immigration Act 96
computers 105
Concorde 76, 108
Conservative governments 13, 17, 27, 33, 49, 53, 59, 67, 75, 80, 86, 100, 105
Conservative Party 7, 16, 47–48, 64, 66, 70, 74, 80, 84–85, 136
Coronation 50–51
Cotton, Billy 144
coupons 122 (see also *rationing* and *clothes*)
Cousins, Frank 66
Coventry 115, 132
Craig, Donald 134
credit squeeze 67–68, 71
cricket 116–117
crime 131–136
Cripps, Sir Stafford 10–11, 45–46, 68, 89, 122
Crosby, Bing 138, 143
Crosland, Anthony 17, 65

Crossman, Richard 65
Croydon 115
CSE 99
Cuba 86
Cyprus 85, 93
Czechoslovakia 82

Dales, the 104
Dalton, Hugh 13
Deakin, Arthur 89
death penalty 134
Decca 145
Declaration of Intent 68
delinquency (juvenile) 131–136
demobilisation 11, 123
dentists 22, 45
depressed areas 24–25, 28, 62
Depression (1930s) 24, 93
Derby (Epsom) 50
devaluation 11, 47, 68–69
Devlin, Bernadette 140
Dior 121–123
discotheques 145
divorce 130, 147
doctors 21–22, 94
Donnison Report 103
Douglas aircraft 108
Douglas, J. W. B. 102
drugs 139, 149
Dulles, J. F. 82
Dylan, Bob 138, 143

Eccles, David 38
Eden, Sir Anthony 64–65, 84
education 58, 95, 98–103, 138, 150
Edwards, Jimmy 104
Egypt 9, 82–84
elections
 1945 7
 1950 47, 50
 1951 17, 47–48, 51, 64
 1959 53, 59, 65, 72, 93
 1964 66, 74, 80
 1966 74
 1970 69, 74
electrical engineers 100
electric trains 110
electronics 57
eleven plus examination 102–103
Elizabeth II, Queen 49–50, 121–122, 140
Ellis, Ruth 134–135
EMI 145
emigrants 94
Empire, British 29–33, 47, 81–86, 150
Empire, Dutch and French 30
employment 24–28, 51–53, 58–60, 62, 90, 93
Employment and Productivity, Ministry of 127, 150
Employment, White Paper on (1944) 24, 88
entertainment 104, 112–117, 141–145
equal pay 127
Eton 98
European Coal and Steel Community 77
European Economic Community (Common Market) 75, 77–80
European Free Trade Area 75, 79
European Parliament 77
Europe, United 75
evacuation 18–19, 133
Evans, Timothy 134
Everest, Mount 50
exports 9, 11, 25, 34, 70–71, 77, 81, 89, 142

family income 60, 63, 126
family planning 129–30
family, size of 63, 128
Farouk, King 33, 82
fashion 121–123

Festival of Britain 36–37, 49
Festival Hall 38
films 112–113, 145, 148
Fleming, Sir Alexander 100
food tastes 119–120 (see also *rationing*)
football 116, 148
Ford Motor Company 28, 57
Free Trade Area 79
fuel crisis (1947) 35, 60

Gaitskell, Hugh 46, 64–66, 79
gambling 113, 147–148
Gandhi 29, 30
Gasperi (Italy) 75
Gatwick 108
de Gaulle 66, 70, 73, 77, 78–80
Gaza 83–85
GCE 97, 102
General Strike 87
George V, King 49
George VI, King 8, 49
Germany 39, 40
Ghana (Gold Coast) 85
Glasgow 101
Glubb, Sir John 81
Gollancz, Victor 134
Gordon Walker, Patrick 96
grammar schools 98–103
grants 99
Great Train Robbery 132–133
Greece 41, 118, 120
Griffiths, James 19
Griffiths, Peter 96
Grimethorpe 14
Guildford College of Art 140
guitar groups 141
Gunter, Ray 69
Gunther, John 25, 58, 60, 62, 98

Hair 147
Haldane, Lord 100
Haley, Bill 142
Hancock, Tony 104
Hanoi 80
Harben, Philip 106
Harlow 52–53
Havilland, Geoffrey de 107–108
Health Service 20, 23, 62
Heath, Edward 74, 78, 80, 136
Heathrow Airport 109
Heath, Ted 141
Herz 31
Hillary, Sir Edmund 50
Hippies 139
hire purchase 61–62
Hitler 81, 152
Hogg, Quintin 48, 73–74, 139
Holbrook 138
holidays 118–120
Home, Sir Alec Douglas 74
Homicide Act 135
homosexuality 146–148
Hornsey College of Art 140
hospitals 19–23, 45
housing, council 26, 53–56
housing points 54
housing shortage 8, 34, 52–55, 95, 137
Hovercraft 109
Howerd, Frankie 104
Hungary 116
Hussein, King 81
Hyde Park 145

Ibos 85–86
ICI 28, 57
illegitimacy 130, 149
immigration 93–99

Immigration Act 96
Imperial College 100–101
imports 8, 44–45, 50–51, 54, 68, 70–71, 74, 77, 81
income, family 60, 63, 126
income, national 68, 72, 79, 138
incomes policy 87
India 9, 29–31, 33, 49, 81, 95, 128
Indonesia 31
Industrial Reorganisation Commission 17, 68
industries, new 57–58, 60, 100, 126, 137–138, 145
industry—aircraft 17
industry, location of 62
infant mortality rates 22–23
inflation 26, 44–45, 68, 75, 90
insurance benefits 20
insurance payments 18, 20
International Monetary Fund 71, 79
Isle of Wight 138, 143
Israel 32, 82, 84, 128
ITA 105
Italy 75, 77, 113, 118, 120

Jamaica 84, 95
Jay, Douglas 69
Jenkins, Roy 148–149, 153
jet engine 108
Jews 31–32, 95
Jinnah 30
Jordan 81
jumbo jet 109

Kennedy, J. F. (President) 80, 86, 152
Kenya 50, 85
Keynes, J. M. 9, 13
Kidbrooke School 103
Korea 36, 38, 42, 44, 50, 89
Kruschev 86

Labour governments
 1945–50 8, 19, 33, 45, 52, 89
 1950 45–47
 1964–70 67–68, 75, 80, 86, 92, 97, 103, 120, 148
Labour Party 7, 17, 19, 47, 49, 64–67, 74, 79, 90, 93, 96
Lady Chatterley's Lover 146
Lancaster 100
Landy, John 116
Lane, Judge Elizabeth 128
Lane, Sir Allen 115–117
launderettes 58, 146
Laver, James 124
law and order 136
law reforms 134–136
Lawrence, D. H. 146
LEAs 103
Lease-Lend 9
Leatherhead 115
Lee, Miss Jennie 115
Leicester Plan 103
Librarians 126
Littlewood, Miss Joan 113
Lloyd George 7, 21
Lloyd, Selwyn 72, 88, 90
local government officers 90, 126
London 132
London County Council 103
London School of Economics 140
London, Swinging 114
Look Back in Anger 114, 122
Loss, Joe 141
Luxembourg 77
Lynn, Vera 141

MacArthur, General 42–43
Macleod, Iain 48
Macmillan, Harold 26–27, 59, 64, 66, 69–70, 72,
 74, 77, 79–80, 88, 95, 152
Majorca 120
Malawi 86
Malaya 85
Malta 93, 119
Manchester 101
Mao Tse Tung 42–43
Marconi 109
Marks and Spencer's 53, 58–59, 121
Marshall Aid 9–10, 48, 76, 81
Marshall Plan 41
Marvin, Lee 145
Maudling, Reginald 48, 74, 79
MCC 66
Messina (Italy) 77
middle class 19, 62, 66, 90–91, 102, 117–118, 138–139
Midlands 93, 95, 97
mini-skirts 114
Mollisons, the 107
Monnet, Jean 77
Montgomery, Field Marshal 40
Morrison, Herbert 8, 16, 37, 88
Mosley, Sir Oswald 93, 95
Mossadeq 33
mothers, unmarried 130
mothers, working 115, 126–129, 133
motor car and crime 132
motor car ownership 110–111, 132
motor car production 57, 110
motorways 111
Mountbatten, Lord Louis 30

Nassau 80
Nasser, Colonel (President) 82–83
National Assistance Act 18
National Coal Board 13–14, 28
National Economic Development Council 72–73
National Health Service 19–23, 62
national income 68, 72, 79, 138
National Incomes Commission 71
National Insurance 18–19, 21, 24
National Insurance Act 18–21, 24
nationalisation 12–17, 65–66, 89
 (see also *coal*, *British Railways*)
nationalisation of Suez Canal 64, 82–84
National Plan 67–68
National Service 44, 132
NATO 42, 47, 76, 81
Nehru, Pandit 30
New Look 122–124
newspapers 107, 145
New Towns 52, 54, 56
New Zealand 29, 78, 94
Nigeria 85–86, 95, 140
Nixon, President 136
N'krumah, Kwame 85
Northern Ireland 140
North Kensington 93, 95
Nottingham 115
Notting Hill 95
nuclear disarmament 66–67, 152
nuclear weapons 69, 152
nudity in films 147
nurses 71, 90–91, 94
Nyasaland 86

Ogilvie, Vivian 104
Oh, Calcutta! 114–115, 147
d'Oliveira, Basil 117
Olympic Games 115
opinion polls 65, 69, 146
Organisation for European Economic Cooperation 76–77
Osborne, John 114, 122
Oxfam 152
Oxford University 115, 140

Paish, Professor 26
Pakistan 29–30, 81
Palestine 30
paperbacks 115
parking meters 111
participation 153
participation by students 140, 151
participation by workers 151
pay pause 88, 90
Peers, Donald 141
Penguin Books 115, 147
pensions 18, 29, 69
permissive society 133, 139, 146–149
Persia 32-33, 38
Philip, Prince 121–122, 140
pill 129–130
Pinter 119
Pirie, Gordon 115
Plan, National 67–68
Polaris 69, 80
police 131–132, 148, 151
Polytechnics 100–101
poor 62–63
pop fans 104, 124, 142
pop music 104, 141–145
pop records 104, 142–145
pop stars 138, 142
Port Said 83
post-War reconstruction 88
Powell, Enoch 48, 64, 91, 96, 140
prescription charges 23, 45
Presley 141, 146
prices 60, 88, 90
Prices and Incomes Board 68–69, 90, 150
Priestley, J. B. 62
prisons 135–136
productivity 68–69
Profumo, John 73–74
punishment 134–136

Quant, Mary 123–124, 137

Race Relations Act 97
race riots 95
Rachman 56
radio 104
railways 110 (see also *British Railways, nationalisation*)
Ramadhin 116
rationing 10, 34, 36, 44, 47–48, 122, 124
Ray, Johnny 138, 143
rearmament 44–45
records 114–115, 141, 144–145
Redundancy Payment Act 27
Rent Act 56, 69
rent control 56
Retraining Act 27
Rhodesia 69, 86, 140
Richards, Gordon 50
Ridleagh, Miss Mabel 122
road transport 110
rockets 104, 109
Rolling Stones 142–145
Rome, Treaty of 78–79
Royal Court Theatre 113–114, 122
Russell, Bertrand 152
Russia 38–39, 42, 44, 66, 69, 76, 81–82, 84–86, 128
Rutherford, Lord 17

Samuels, Lord 106
school leavers 97
schools 54, 73, 98–103, 113, 151
schools, comprehensive 99, 103
Schumann, Robert 75, 77
scientists, applied 100–101
Scotland 150

Sèvres 83
Shaw, Sandie 143
Shelter 152–153
Shinwell, Emmanuel 79
shops 51, 58–59, 119, 125–126, 132, 145
Short, Edward 97
Sierra Leone 85
Silverman, Sidney 134
Sinatra, Frank 143
skiffle 140–141
Skinheads 138–139
Smethwick 96
Smith, Ian 86
Social Security 18, 20, 22, 27, 89
social services 46, 72, 95
South Africa 46, 69, 140
South African cricket and rugby tours 117
Spaak 77
space research 104, 109
spiv 36
sport 115–117
Springfield, Dusty 143
Squatters 54–55
Stalin 39–41
standard of living 89–90, 94, 125–126, 137
Stapleton, Cyril 41
steel 16–17, 57
Steele, Tommy 141, 146
Stock Exchange 8
strikes 14–15, 68, 74, 90–92, 151
students 64, 138, 140, 151
Sudan 85
Suez Canal 33, 70, 81–84
Suez invasion (1956) 64–65
supersonic speed 107
Sussex, University of 140
Swan, Sir Joseph 100

Tanganyika 85
tariffs 77, 79
Tawney, R. H. 60, 98, 103
taxation 45
tax, direct (income) 45, 94
tax, indirect 94
tax, purchase 45, 120, 124
teachers 71, 91, 94–96, 126–128
technology 58, 100–101
Technology, Manchester College of 100
Technology, Ministry of 150
Teddy Boys 122–123
teenagers 114, 124, 137–140, 143–145
television 65, 104–107, 115, 133
television, BBC 106
television, commercial 65, 105
television companies 105, 106
television licences 105
television sets 51, 55, 61, 93, 104–105, 112
terms of trade 44
theatre 113–114
Thorneycroft, Peter 48, 64
Tiger, HMS 86
tourist agencies 118–120
tourists 119
tourists and balance of payments 119
tourists, foreign 119
trade unions 45, 67–68, 70–71, 74, 87–92, 118, 125
Trade Union Congress 88–89, 92, 127
transistors 104
transport 110–111
Truman Doctrine 41, 48
Truman, Harry 32, 42–43
Tulloh, Bruce 115
turbo-jet 106–108
Turkey 31
Tynan, Kenneth 147
Tyneside 28

unemployed, Beveridge and 19, 24
unemployed, post-War 26, 64
unemployed, pre-War 7, 13, 24
unemployed, 1962–63 27, 72
universities 100–101, 138, 150
UNO 32, 40, 42–43, 69, 84–86
USA 38, 49, 66, 69, 80–81, 94, 106 (see *America*)

Valentine 116
Vassall 73
Vatican 113
Victorian 148
Vietnam 140

wage inflation 71, 88, 90
wage-related benefits 69
wages 60, 62, 93, 95, 132
wages and affluence 90
wages freeze 45, 71, 89
wages policy 88–90
wages, rising 60, 68, 70, 72, 88, 90
Waiting for Godot 114
Walcott, Clyde 117
Wales 151
Walker-Smith, Sir Derek 79
War
   (1914–18) 7, 81
   (1939–45) 7–8, 81, 125, 137
   (Cold) 39–40
   (Korean) 36, 38–44, 50, 89
Warwick 100, 140
Washington 86
Weekes, Everton 117
Weinstock, Arnold 17
welfare clinics 19
welfare services 18
Welfare State 18–25, 52–56, 66, 90, 150, 153
Wesker 114
West Indies 93, 116–117
Whittle, Sir Frank 51, 108
Williams, Francis 12–13, 50
Wilson, Des 152
Wilson, Harold 10, 44–45, 47, 65–67, 69, 72, 74, 78–80, 137
wireless 104, 115
Wolfenden, Sir John 146
Wolfson, Sir Isaac 61
Wolverhampton 97
women and fashion 121–124
women, unmarried 116
women and wages 125
women in wartime 125
women workers 60, 125–129
Woodcock, George 89–90
Woolton, Lord 48, 100
workers 25, 58, 60, 62, 98, 138
workers and changing home life 55, 62
workers and expectations 58–59, 62, 137
workers as property owners 61
workers, status of 91
workers, unskilled 95 (see also *coloured immigrants and workers*)
workers, women 60, 125
World Cup 116
Worrell 117

yachting 117–118
Yalta 39
Yeats, W. B. 153
Yippies 139
York 100
Yorkshire 95
Youth Employment Officer 97, 102
Yugoslavia 120

Zambia 86
Zanzibar 85
Zen Buddhism 139, 146
Zweig, Ferdynand 62, 126, 128

Soc
DA
566.4
L3